CENTRIFUGE™
YOUTH MINISTRY
SOURCEBOOK

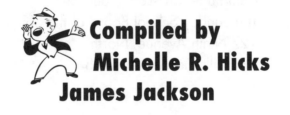 **Compiled by
Michelle R. Hicks
James Jackson**

**Convention Press
Nashville, Tennessee**

©Copyright 1997 Convention Press. All rights reserved.
5200-91
ISBN 07673-1973-7
259.23
Centrifuge/Youth Ministry

Printed in the United States of America
Centrifuge/Crosspoint Section
The Sunday School Board of the Southern Baptist Convention
127 Ninth Avenue, North
Nashville, Tennessee 37234

Table of Contents

Introduction and Acknowledgments

For three years, from 1992-1994, I served as a camp pastor In the Centrifuge program. During those years, I led the Youth Ministry Roundtable track time, primarily because I was too athletically challenged to lead softball, the traditional choice for many Centrifuge camp pastors. The idea was simple: Get a bunch of youth leaders together for an hour each day, and let them talk about stuff. Put tear sheets up on the wall, with headings like "Fund Raisers," "Creative Bible Studies," "Fellowships and Games," "Mission and Service Projects," "Programming to Respond to Youth Needs," and "Issues Your Youth Face." Throw a lot of markers on the floor and then watch the youth workers go after them like dogs after raw meat, as they scramble to put their ideas up on the sheets. You see, I realized that, as a young seminary student at that time, there wasn't much I could teach a roomful of seasoned, in-the-trenches youth workers. Their job during the week was to spill gasoline on the floor. My job was to hold the matches and see what discussions we could ignite.

What you hold in your hands now is an extension of that project. After those summers, the good folks who run Centrifuge took the project to all the camps, soliciting contributions from folks everywhere. Some of the ideas in here are more fleshed-out than others. Some are really off the wall (Cow-Pie Bingo comes to mind), while others are variations on tried-and-true themes, such as bake sales, car washes, and object lessons. All of them came from ministers and youth workers in local churches of various sizes and locales. But none of them is a prepackaged, ready-to-go idea that you can simply plug-and-play into your situation. Because each setting is different, these ideas need to serve merely as a launching pad, not the moon itself.

With the advent of online information services, there has been an additional wellspring of ideas. Many of the ideas listed here were downloaded from SBCNet, a service available through Compuserve. If you have not yet taken an on ramp to the information superhighway, I would encourage you to do so. It's like having a Youth Ministry Roundtable every day of the year!

So like I said, I didn't write this book. The folks listed here did. If your name is listed here, thanks for sharing. I am a youth minister now, and my loose-leaf notebook of ideas occupies a prominent place on my shelf. I've used a lot of your ideas already.
Thanks to my wife, Trish, for looking over my shoulder, helping me sort ideas, and being infinitely patient during the writing process. Thanks also to my youth group, for being guinea pigs on a lot of these ideas.

It is my prayer that, just as they did during the summers at Youth Ministry Roundtable, these ideas will spark other ideas, which will spark other ideas, and so on, and so on...

James Jackson
FBC Kingsport, TN

Although this is not my first book, it is always exciting to work on any project which will enhance someone's youth ministry. So this book is for all those faithful ministers who constantly strive to build relationships with youth and lead them to the living and true God. You are definitely investing your life in something which will outlast it. My prayer is that through the crazy games, the wild fellowships, the fund-raising, the creative Bible studies, and the mission and service projects, youth and their leaders will grow closer to one another and stronger in their relationship with Christ. May we all glorify God and experience the abundant life we have in Christ through the ideas in this book.

Michelle R. Hicks
Franklin, TN

Fund-raising Ideas

Fund-raisers. Like them or loathe them, they are a part of almost every youth ministry on the planet. Let's face it. Youth ministry programming is expensive. Because we live in a "bigger and better" culture, youth are often not satisfied unless this year's camp tops last year's, the mission trip goes farther away, or the ski trip finds a better slope. This says nothing about weekly programming. The more high-tech, low-attention-span our world gets, the more youth ministry is in danger of getting left in the dust. Often, student ministries find themselves in need of better (and more expensive) equipment.

Enter the fund-raiser. Different churches have different ideas about how much or how little of them you can do. Some say none at all. There are some thoughts about that in this chapter. Some are so sick of fund-raisers that they would rather just give you money outright. So, there are some creative ideas about that in here, too. Hopefully, you will glean some useful ideas that you can adapt to whatever your situation is.

"But My Church Doesn't Allow Fund-raisers..."

For various reasons, some very good, many churches do not allow fund-raisers. The first thing for a youth worker to do is find out why. For some, it is an issue of pride. The church doesn't want the impression in the community that it does not take care of its own. Others want their youth to understand how the unified church budget works; they plan for the budget to fund all youth events. Still others equate fund-raising with having

money-changers in the temple. On the other end of the spectrum, one youth worker complained that it seemed all his group ever did was fund-raising. "We do so many car washes that it seems like we are letting opportunities for ministry pass by."

How do you deal with these concerns? One of the great advantages to allowing youth to raise money for various activities is that it gives them ownership in the program. If you are fund-raising for capital expenses, youth are more likely to take care of the things they have worked for.

Here are some alternatives and random thoughts on fund-raising that many say have worked in their churches:

❶ Look closely at the things you are asking money for. Fund-raising toward a mission trip will have greater success than fund-raising toward a theme park trip.

❷ A free car wash. Community members will often donate money anyway when they realize who you are. Often, a car wash promoted as "Donations Accepted" will raise more money than those with a set price.

❸ Check with people in the church, particularly senior adults, about scholarships or sponsorships for youth activities.

❹ Find ministry opportunities that also happen to bring in money. For example, a Parents' Night Out for the community does a great service for young parents in your town and can bring in funds at the same time.

❺ If your youth ministry has a performing group such as puppets, clowning, drama, or band, make yourself available to perform for other churches. Love

offerings and honorariums are a good source of income, and your youth are doing real ministry.

6 If the fund-raiser can be linked to a project or an event so that it isn't just fund-raising for fund-raising's sake (e.g., selling light bulbs), then the church may be more receptive to it. Many churches with youth drama groups present dinner or dessert theaters. Your group has come together by working on the project, and they are presenting a message, too. The money is not the primary reward for a project like this.

ANR Banquet

This is basically a solicitation drive for people who are sick of fund-raisers. Have an "Attendance Not Required" banquet. Sell tickets, but let people know there won't be any food or entertainment, and they are not required to show up.

Arts and Crafts Fair

Plan an arts and crafts fair for your community. This event can be held at your church parking lot, a local park, or another visible place in the community. Make sure you receive the proper permission for your location, and advertise the fair well. Be careful of the date you pick for the arts and crafts fair. Make sure it is not at the same time as a big game or other community event.

Allow people to register their booths in advance and pay a fee for the space. You may want to sell the items on a consignment basis. This way the youth group receives a portion of the profit made on the items. Some people may donate their craft items to the sale.

Bake-less Bake Sale

This is a new twist on an old idea. At the end of the worship service, youth stand at the exits of the sanctuary holding empty cake mix boxes, empty frosting tins, and so on. Youth ask for donations for the cost of the ingredients. If you have ever had a youth group parent tell you, "If I have to buy one more light bulb, box of candy, case of oranges, roll of wrapping paper, or calendar, I am going to pull my hair out. I'd rather just give the money outright," then this idea could work at your church. (This idea might have come from the same church that suggested the ANR Banquet!)

Bake Sale at a Bank

This is smart. Set up a table selling brownies and cookies outside a bank on Fridays. People are more likely to buy stuff after they have cashed their pay checks. Make sure you have permission from the bank to set up your table.

Balloon-a-Gram

Here is a great Valentine's Day idea. Youth put together baskets with Mylar balloons, foil-wrapped chocolate drops, a teddy bear, and a personalized message. They sold them for $6, or $7 delivered. Expenses for the project were around $700, and the profits were around $1,400. One thing that helped to keep the expenses down was having connections within the church. Floral shops gave discounts, and the helium was donated. If the youth are allowed to make a pitch during the deacons' meeting, you should have good success, especially if the deacons' meeting is just a few days before Valentine's Day.

Bigger and Better Yard Sale

This is a fun way to collect items for a church yard sale. Give pairs of youth a small item, like a pen. Send them door-to-door among church members with this pitch: "I'm collecting items for our church yard sale. So far, all I have is this pen. Can you donate something bigger or better?" Whatever the person gives, youth show that item at the next house. Who knows what they might come back with? ("So far, all I've got is this Lexus...")

Bus Rental

If your church bus sits idle most of the time, consider renting it to other groups and churches. Make sure to check your insurance policy first. You would probably have to furnish a driver. The renting group would pay for lodging for the driver and a fee for bus use.

Buy a Mile

Make a display which plots your route to summer camp. Figure the total number of miles round trip, then divide the total cost of the trip by the total number of miles to get an idea of cost per mile. Color in the road to show your progress toward your goal.

Cake Decorating Contest and Auction

Divide youth into pairs. Provide cake mixes and decorating supplies. Ask the teams to design, bake, and decorate a cake of their choice. Place all the cakes on a table, each with a number. Let the large group vote on the cakes (decoration only) and award a winner. Then take the cakes to a church event and auction them off. The money raised can be used for missions or another youth event.

Car Crash

Please be sure to get the proper approval for this fund raiser! Begin by procuring an old car from a salvage yard. You will probably need to have the car towed to your designated "crash" site. Make sure to remove any glass or metal which could be a safety hazard. Enlist several adults to help with supervision of the car crash event.

At the time of the event, provide marker and other supplies. Ask youth to write on and decorate the car. This is just a fun time for the group to be together. Then for one dollar per person (or another specific amount) youth or adults may "crash and smash" the car with a mallet. Make sure no more than two or three youth are swinging mallets at one time. All the proceeds go to a designated fund or missions offering.

Church Custodians

Custodians are usually hard to find and often underpaid. However, your group can work together to raise money as well as to provide a service for your church or for another local church. Begin by enlisting churches in your area who need a cleaning service. Divide youth into small cleaning teams and organize specific cleaning days. With a good sized group, the job can be done in a short time. This can give your group a constant source for raising funds and an avenue of service as well.

Collecting Phone Books

There are many telephone companies who pay for recycling phone books. Check on the possibility of the phone company in your area providing this service. Ask youth to collect phone books during a designated month. Turn all the phone books in and collect your cash for recycling!

Cookbooks

Get recipes from church members. Find a fund-raising company that publishes cookbooks. Your cookbooks will come back nicely bound, with even a "Recipe for Life" plan of salvation on the inside front cover.

Note: With the improved quality and lower price of computer desk-top publishing programs, one church found they could make more money putting the book together themselves.

Cow-Pie Bingo

A rancher in one church divided his cow pasture into a 25 square grid with each square about 10 feet on a side. Church members "bought" one or more grid squares. Then, as part of a church-wide fellowship at the farm, the rancher released a cow into the pasture. The "owner" of the square in which the cow "made her deposit" won a prize. It's a bizarre idea, but this church had a great time with it. Udderly amazing!

Creative Publishing

Have the youth group write their own book. Instruct youth to write stories, poems, and articles. In addition to writing, the students may draw inspirational pictures or cartoons. Assign a committee to edit everything. Have the book pasted up and printed by an offset printer. Then have a printer or bindery bind the submitted material into a book. Advertise the books and sell them in the church or community. Here is another place your desktop publishing system can save you money.

Dime-a-Dip Dinner

Youth plan a food-tasting event where all the food is prepared or donated by your members. (You may be able to get local bakeries or restaurants to donate food.) People are invited to attend, paying a dime for every sample of food they put on their plate or in their mouth. Everything costs a dime, including drinks, appetizers, pats of butter, single chips, or individual crackers. The response is usually great if it is advertised as a benefit dinner or tasting. If possible, provide some form of entertainment or a speaker to help draw a larger crowd. Be sure to have lots of dimes on hand to make change.

Easter Egg Sale

You begin by going door to door among church members, asking the person there if he or she will donate an egg to help your youth group earn money. Youth will need to explain what they will be doing with the eggs and where the money will go. Usually anyone will give an egg. After youth have collected their eggs, they return

to the church or someone's home. After preparing the eggs (by blowing out the contents), youth decorate the eggs for Easter. The only expense will be the cost of the decorating materials. After the eggs are decorated, youth go door to door selling the eggs. They may also sell the eggs at church or at a local elementary school. The eggs can be sold for from twenty-five cents to a dollar. If the decorating materials were donated, all money made is profit

.

Exams Survival Kit

Purchase small gift boxes and fill them with items for students to use during a week of exams. Survival items might include gum, aspirin, granola bar, candy, instant hot chocolate, facial tissues, tea bags, pencils, and so forth. The survival kits can be sold at schools, or to parents and friends. Some parents may want to send one to their son or daughter at college. If the survival items are donated, you can keep the expenses down. The Exams Survival Kit may become an annual tradition with graduating seniors receiving one as they leave for college.

Fast Food Partnership

One youth minister had a great deal going with the Burger King in his town. On Monday nights, Burger King gave twenty percent of its receipts to the youth group. In return, the youth group brought in business for what had always been a dead night for Burger King, anyway. Burger King became the Monday night place to be. The restaurant also let this youth group promote a "Free Whopper with Car Wash" day in their parking lot, and the group made about $1,600 on this event.

Food Sales.

Brunswick Stew: One church with a killer recipe sold the stuff. The youth had parents brown ground beef and bring it to the church. They cooked the stew in huge pots, and sold it by the gallon ($12/gallon, and the purchasers brought their own containers). This particular church sold out of their 200 gallons quickly.

Barbecued Chicken: Another church did basically the same thing with barbecued chicken. One church smoked turkeys before Thanksgiving and Christmas, and sold them for $15. Local grocery stores even donated or offered items at a discount.

Cakes to Order: Take orders for a variety of different cakes, then bake them and deliver when they are still warm.

Super Bowl Sub Sale: Youth took advance orders for sub sandwiches on Super Bowl Sunday. They put them together after church that day, then delivered them to people in time for the game.

Easter Sunrise Service Breakfast: One group sold tickets for a breakfast held after a community Easter sunrise service.

Carry-out Lunches for business people. During the summer, one group sold barbecue carry-out to business persons in the community. They found the most success with delivering to auto dealerships, where salespeople didn't like going out to lunch because they might miss a sale.

Any time you are doing any type of food sale, check with the Health Department in your area. One church had an incredible idea to sell venison during deer season, only to find out later that it was illegal. Do your homework!

Harold the Flamingo

This one is a blast to do. If you have a church with a playful spirit and members who live in fairly close proximity to one another, you can have a lot of fun with this one. Harold is a pink plastic lawn flamingo whose migration habits tend to bring him into your area right before your youth mission trip.

Three weeks before the fund-raiser, the youth put signs all over the church: "Harold's Coming!"

Two weeks before, the signs got more specific: "Harold the Flamingo is landing [date]!"

One week before, youth went to adult Sunday School classes, with Harold in hand, to explain the game to folks. If a church member woke one morning to find Harold in the front lawn, they were asked to give a $10 donation to the youth group for the care and feeding of Harold. Then they were asked to help Harold find a new home (someone else in the church). However, if they got caught transplanting Harold, they had to pay another $5. (The group explained that Harold got traumatized very easily, and this $5 was to offset therapy expenses!) The youth printed a bright pink bulletin insert with all the rules on one side. On the other side was a sign for church members to put in their window or on their door saying, "PLEASE, NO FLAMINGOS." The group wanted to give people the option not to play if they didn't want to. In the three weeks the game was played, Harold was the talk of the Fellowship Hall. Stories would come in about the pastor getting caught in the chairman of the deacons' yard at three in the morning with Harold under his arm. At the end of the game, the youth had raised over $300, but more importantly, they taught the church to play together. Harold became an annual event.

Kiss a Pig

If you have an annual church picnic or hayride, this idea works well. Several weeks beforehand, make a display of each church

PLEASE NO FLAMINGOS!!

staff member's picture on a jar. (Each Sunday School department could have its own set of jars.) People vote for which staff member they want to see kiss a pig at the annual picnic by putting money into that jar.

Lawn-a-Thon

Enlist as many youth as possible with lawn mowers and transportation for each of them. Advertise that on a specific Saturday the group will be mowing lawns for free. Ask youth to get as many people as possible to sign up to have their lawn mowed. Each youth also carries a pledge sheet to take pledges (twenty-five cents, one dollar, and so on) for every lawn mowed on the set date. After the big Saturday event, youth can go and collect their pledge money. It is not only a great fund-raiser, but also a service to the community neighborhoods.

Lip-Sync Contest

This is like a talent show except the groups perform lip-sync acts. Several weeks in advance advertise the contest and prepare cassette tapes to be used by the groups. It is best to select the tapes yourself to make sure all entries are appropriate. Let the groups choose a tape and begin to practice their act during their free time. The lip-sync contest can also be used at a camp or retreat. At the time of the event charge a fee both for those who participate and those who just come to watch the contest. Explain that the funds raised will go to missions or another designated purpose (helping to send youth to camp, for example).

Make Your Own Christmas Cards

As a youth group, design your own Christmas cards. These can be very simple or elaborate. Possibly someone in the group will have access to a computer with card-making capabilities. Package the cards in bundles of five, ten, fifteen, twenty, and twenty-five. Sell the

cards to members of the congregation or in the community. The money can then be given to the missions offering or used where needed.

March Madness Basketball Tournament

Organize a community-wide, inter-school, three-on-three basketball tournament for high school boys, using your church gym. Charge a $10 per team entry fee, and get refer-ees to donate their time. Make sure you use league-sanctioned refer-ees so that the tourna-ment will be credible enough to attract fairly good players. Plan the tournament to coincide with the NCAA Tournament in March, and draw up brackets just like the NCAA's. If you play half-court games to twenty and use both halves of  your church gym, you could easily do the first round on a Friday night and Saturday, and all successive rounds on Saturdays. This tournament could also be an excellent outreach for your church.

Matching Funds Programs

Check with your local super center department store. In some areas, superstore chains like Wal-Mart and Target offer matching funds programs. If you have a car wash or bake sale in their park-ing lot, they match the money you make up to a certain dollar amount.

Mega-Maze

This is an exciting fund-raiser and a great alternative to use instead of Halloween options. Ask youth to collect large appliance boxes (refrigerator cartons are best) several weeks in advance. Locate a

large room or garage to use where most furniture and other items can be totally removed. Using the boxes, assorted tables, and duct tape, build a giant maze. Be creative with the design, allowing for plenty of dead ends and trap doors. Advertise the Mega-Maze in the community. Planned for and used around Halloween, it is fun for all ages and a great alternative to haunted houses. Of course, the proceeds may be used for the youth group or for another designated offering.

Missions Carnival

This is your basic carnival except all the proceeds go to missions. Begin by planning the booths you would like to have available. Delegate the various booths to small groups or Sunday school classes. Each group is responsible for soliciting donations for prizes and the actual supplies needed for the booth. The small groups will also decorate their booth and make sure there is someone there to run the booth during the carnival. The carnival will be even better if a stage can be set up where music and drama are performed periodically. Just like an actual carnival, provide ticket booths. This will help eliminate problems with money and making change at the individual booths. Instead, post signs stating the number of tickets needed to participate at that particular booth. Possible booths include dunking booth, football throw, golf putt, goldfish bowl, ring toss, softball throw, darts and balloons, bobbing for apples, egg throw. The carnival can be as large or as small as needed, depending on the size of the church or youth group.

Money Mania

Money Mania works best at a camp or Vacation Bible School. Ask youth to bring a certain denomination of coin each day or night during the worship services. When it is time for the offering, follow this plan.

Monday: <u>Nickel</u> <u>Night.</u> Each person gives one nickel for every letter in the giver's full name.

Tuesday: <u>Quarter</u> <u>Night.</u> One quarter for every member of his or her family.

Wednesday: <u>Dime</u> <u>Night.</u> One dime for every finger and thumb on the giver.

Thursday: <u>Penny</u> <u>Night</u>. One penny for every pound the giver weighs.

Friday: <u>Dollar</u> <u>Night.</u> One dollar for a life and heart saved by Jesus.

You may use this mania idea to raise money for missions or as an offering for another special need. This is really fun, and everyone seems to enjoy giving in this way. (Be careful that no youth feels he has to stay away if he doesn't have the money.) Make sure you enlist volunteers to help roll the coins into wrappers, a huge task for one person.

Money Tree

This church cut a small sapling and put it in a prominent display area. They bought cardboard apples from a school supply store, and wrote various denominations on the apples— some $5, some $10, $20, $50, and so on. People who wanted to support the youth ministry picked the apple of their choice and bought it. The idea appealed to the church, because they liked having a visual indication toward a specific goal.

Mother's Day Dinner

Mother's Day is the busiest day of the year for restaurants. One church realized this, and the youth sold advance tickets to a Mother's Day dinner after the morning worship service. The church loved it, because they didn't have to fight the crowds at local restaurants. The youth acted as servers and even presented mothers with a rose.

One consideration to keep in mind: the youth are pulled out of the worship service (and possibly Sunday School, too) in order to get this ready. The more you can do to set up on Saturday, the less this will be a problem, but it is still something to bear in mind.

Multiplying Your Talents

As an object lesson on the parable of the talents, give each youth a dollar bill and one month to make it grow. They may do whatever they wish with the dollar bill. They may invest it, spend it, save it; however, at the end of the month they must account for their one dollar (or "talent"). During the month discuss stewardship and multiplying our gifts for God. The money earned during the month has not only taught a lesson but also raised more money for a worthy cause.

Newsletter Subscriptions

As a youth group, take subscriptions for a monthly newsletter. Make sure the subscription amount covers the costs involved plus any unexpected expenses. Ask youth to volunteer to write specific parts of the newsletter. Possible ideas include devotional thoughts, memory verse of the month, youth group news, church news, what's happening in the world, a listing of the top ten contemporary Christian songs, cartoons, and so on. Instruct youth to lay out the newsletter at a designated time each month. Have a group edit the newsletters. Print them and then mail or hand out on a given day.

Newspaper Recycling Bin

Depending on your community, the church can often keep all or part of the money from recycling newspapers if they simply put the recycling bin in a corner of the church parking lot.

Parade Clean-up

Contract with your local parade organizer, stadium, or fairgrounds to do clean-up after a major event. The job usually takes several days but can earn lots of money. Organize youth into specific teams with certain jobs. This makes the task faster and less overwhelming. It seems like a lot of work, but when the money is earned, it is all worth it.

Penny War

Have two big watercooler jars, one for girls, one for guys (or go by Sunday School departments, grades, high schools represented in your group, whatever). Each penny counts as a positive point; each one of the other coins counts as a negative point. So teams are putting large amounts of loose change into the other team's jar. At the end of the playing time, the losing team serves the winning team dinner.

Personality-Driven Fund-raisers

Often, you can set a fund-raising goal tied to your personality. A youth minister with really long hair would cut it if the youth raised a certain amount of money and would get a flat top if they raised a certain amount more. Another used the Penny War concept (see Penny War), for the youth group to vote on whether he should save his goatee or shave it. One group brought in a professional wrestler for the pastor to take on if the group raised a certain amount.

In one church, the pastor wanted to lose weight, and people pledged a certain amount per pound for him to lose. (Note that this idea pretty much has to originate with the pastor! It would not bode well for you to suggest it.)

Pizza Hut Buffet

One church sold tickets (two "all you can eat" buffets for $10.00). Pizza Hut set up their catering racks in the fellowship hall, and the entire church enjoyed a very profitable pizza fellowship.

Pumpkin Whomp

This is a great fund-raising event which requires very little work in advance. Publicize the Pumpkin Whomp in the community. Charge a fee for participating or for just watching the event. Explain that pumpkins will be dropped from the church roof and judged in several categories. Please be sure to receive any prior approval needed from church leaders or committees before the event. In advance, purchase pumpkins or have them donated. Since they will be dropped from a roof, they can be odd shaped and bruised. Make a huge target using old sheets or drop clothes.

As people arrive divide them into small groups of no more than twelve. Instruct each group to decorate their pumpkin and name it. Provide plenty of markers, glitter, string, and other supplies for decorating the pumpkins. It would be great to provide refreshments or slices of pumpkin pie. After ample time, ask one representative from each team to come forward with their pumpkin. The pumpkins can be judged on appearance in several categories according to audience applause. Categories may include best looking pumpkin, looks least like a pumpkin, most orange, most creative, and so on.

Instruct each team to send another representative with the pumpkin to the top of the roof. Make sure everyone is escorted safely. One by one, allow the representatives to drop their pumpkins from the top of the roof onto the target. Pumpkins may be judged on: best overall pumpkin whomp, closest to the bull's eye, best spray of pumpkin guts, least amount of damage to the pumpkin (or the audience), and other categories. Award the winners some type of prize.

This is a great fund-raiser to have as an alternative to Halloween activities. Most importantly, make sure you have enlisted plenty of volunteers to help with clean up after the event. Chances are the entire area will need to be hosed down!

Recycling Cans

This is nothing new, but it can be an ongoing fund-raiser with your group. Trash cans labeled for recycling items may be placed at the church, a retreat or camp site, a family life center,

and so forth. The cans are then taken to a recycling center monthly (or weekly if needed), and the money is collected. It may not seem like a lot of money, but it does add up. If the money collected from recycling will send one youth to camp or on a mission trip, it is worth it. (Not to mention the good that recycling does for the environment.)

Road Race

One church organized a Road Race that has become a major event in their community. They held it to go along with their town's Dogwood Festival, so it became the Dogwood Run. There was a 5K and a 10K route. Money was made from entry fees and from company sponsorships. Youth got involved by being at various checkpoints to hand out water to racers. By working with a local track club, this church has made the Dogwood Run a big deal.

Rolling Insurance

About a month before Halloween, start selling insurance policies to church members, promising that if their yard gets "rolled" on Halloween night, the youth will clean it up the next day. One church's youth sold policies for $10.00, and, strangely enough, almost everyone who got insurance also got rolled! The youth enjoyed cleaning it up.

Skate Marathon

Sponsors pay youth so much a mile to skate. You may use rollerblades or roller skates. The goal is for every youth to complete the twenty-six mile course. This may be done in a rented roller rink, determining how many laps make a mile. Youth must skate the laps without stopping. This is an usual event and may even receive some news coverage!

Snow Insurance

Early in the fall, sell snow policies, promising to come shovel the purchaser's sidewalk if it snows. Policies can be sold for various amounts ($10.00 for one time only, $15.00 for two shovelings,

$50.00 for unlimited shovelings, with length of walk taken into consideration.). Depending on where you live, this could be either a no-effort solicitation of funds (in Miami) or a major-effort service project (in Buffalo).

Softball Leagues

If your church has a softball field, there are many opportunities for youth to raise money. If there are no inter-church leagues in your community, set one up, and let a portion of the registration fees go to the youth program. Or let the youth group run a concession stand during the games.

Rent-a-Kid

A classic youth fund-raiser is the concept of hiring out youth to do various jobs for church members. Some churches have set this up as an "auction" time, in which youth are bid on to do odd jobs. While this has been an effective means of raising money for youth events, there are some major points to consider:

✖ Consider the potentially negative messages an "auction" might send to your youth. If a big, football-player type gets sold for fifty dollars in a minute while it takes another youth five minutes to get a bid of ten dollars, it could be devastating.

✖ Are youth getting hired to do equal pay for equal work? Many youth ministers said that their guys complained, "We had to haul dirt, mow grass, and clean garages, and the girls got paid the same for baby-sitting!" Of course, the girls could make the same complaint on the other side!

✖ Does all the money go into one general fund, to be distributed equally among all the youth going on the

trip, or is there a separate account for each youth? If there are separate accounts, what do you do with eleventh-hour decision makers?

One church made the most of the excitement of the auction while avoiding damage to self-esteem by auctioning off services. From a list of services, including pet washing, lawn-mowing, garage cleaning, baby-sitting, house cleaning, and even a gourmet dinner for two, church members bid on what they wanted done. Then the youth minister was able to match number of youth to the size of the task.

Another church did what they called "Centrifuge Employment Agency." The youth minister kept a list of youth who wanted to work to raise money for camp. Church members would call the youth minister when they wanted work to be done.

Service Auctions

Try to get local businesses to donate goods and services, such as a lube job from a local garage, dinner for two at a restaurant, a haircut, a bucket of balls at the driving range, and so forth.

Sports Auctions

If your church is in a metropolitan area with a professional sports team or major college team, write a letter to them asking for help with a church fund-raiser. A church in Dallas auctioned off signed baseball cards from the Rangers, a soccer ball from the Sidekicks, and even a football jersey from the Cowboys, and made big money.

Stock Shares

Sell "shares" in the youth group. One group sold general shares in the summer program for $20 each, another sold $10 mission trip shares. Every quarter, the church had a "stockholders' meeting," which was basically a planning and dreaming session. After the mission trip, stockholders heard the report at a "shareholders' banquet." The purchaser of the stock gets a nice certificate of purchase, a photograph of the youth group, and, if you are selling shares for a mission trip, three postcards from someone on the mission team while they are on the field. For this church, postcard writing was part of the nightly group devotional, and each youth was assigned the names of several shareholders to write to.

Thirty Pieces of Silver

At Easter, ask each youth group member or church member to bring thirty pieces of silver. Any denomination of coin is acceptable, as long as it is silver. Designate the money to a special offering at Easter time.

Thons

Virtually any activity can have "a-thon" appended to it to create a fund-raiser. Simply collect pledges per unit of the activity—per hour, per point, per car, and so on. Here are some ideas to get the creative juices flowing:

* **Jump-a-Thon:** number of jumps or minutes jumped on a jump rope or trampoline. This could be fun on February 29—"Leap Day!"

* **Bowl-a-Thon:** pledges per pin.

* **Rock-a-Thon:** pledges per hour rocked in a rocking chair. This has worked well in a shopping mall setting.

* **Wash-a-Thon:** a free car wash for the community, with youth collecting pledges in the church for number of cars washed. This can work as a double fund-raiser if people are also making donations!

* **Lottie-Thon:** Rent a community sports center for a lock-in, and have youth collect pledges per hour of continuously playing the games that are there— basketball,

racquetball, swimming, chess, whatever. This is fun because it allows youth to do what they enjoy doing, without tying them down to one specific event for twelve hours. (The money for this event went to the Lottie Moon mission offering, hence the name.)

✖ <u>**Walk-a-Thon:**</u> Collect pledges per mile walked.

✖ <u>**Work-a-Thon:**</u> Youth collect pledges per hour worked in the community. Service projects are organized throughout the community, such as picking up trash at city parks or along roads, washing police cars or nursing home vehicles, painting community centers, and so on. There is huge potential for positive and free publicity about your church with this project

✖ <u>**Bible Read-a-Thon:**</u> One church has done this in a lock-in format. They divided the group into thirds, and had each group reading for twenty minutes, while the other two groups had games and fellowship. Another church took Good Friday, when their group was out of school, and, in a seventeen-hour period, read the entire New Testament aloud. They collected pledges per book of the New Testament, with the goal for each youth $1 per book, or $27. They assigned each youth to read for a specific amount of time. Members of the congregation and the community came in throughout the day and night to listen, and the group made cassette tapes of the entire project. Snacks were set up in the fellowship hall for participants.

Chapter Two

Creative Bible Studies

Someone has said, "It is a sin to make the Bible boring." Most of us could not agree more. But we have all seen the brain-dead, glazed-eye gaze of students who just are not connecting to the things we are trying to say. Now if you are like most youth ministers, the shelves in your office are bulging with samples of different curricula. So the ideas here are not fleshed-out studies, complete with three points and a poem. They are merely some ideas for you to tweak.

Animal Talk

Use the characteristics of different animals (snakes, parrots, peacocks, and so on) to illustrate truths.

Around the World

This great idea for a weekly Bible study uses the theme "Around the World." Each week a different country of the world is visited. The room can be decorated to reflect the country and its customs. You may even want to serve native foods of that country as your snack before or after the session. Youth study the population and the impact Christ is having in that country. You may also include studies of various world religions that are predominant in that area of the world. All youth are given a passport at the beginning of the study. Each week their passports are stamped and notes on each country can be stapled into the booklet. This weekly study can incorporate missions projects or activities.

Back-to-School Focus Week

During the week before school starts, plan a Bible study for each night. Each night can have a specific theme which leads into the topic. Be sure to decorate and provide refreshments and allow extra time before or after the Bible study for fellowship. Remember,  this may be the last chance to have the students' full attention for several months! Once classes and extra-curricular activities start, it will be difficult to get youth to commit to anything for five nights in a row. The Bible studies are to help youth prepare spiritually for the school year ahead. Topics may include these.

- ✖ Stand firm in your faith as you face opposition at school.
- ✖ Walk daily with God.
- ✖ Don't leave God in your locker.
- ✖ Be a bold witness for Christ.
- ✖ Be a good steward in your studies.
- ✖ Keep your priorities in order.

Lead youth in a time of commitment at the end of the week. Help youth to commit every area of their lives to God, including the coming school year.

Beautiful Feet

This Bible study focusing on fun foot games also encourages youth to share the good news of Christ. Begin by using various foot games to get the group excited about the subject. For example:

❶ <u>**Feet**</u> <u>**by**</u> <u>**the**</u> <u>**Feet**</u>—Teams line up with their feet in a single file line, heel to toe. The team with the most "footage" wins.

❷ **Foot Drawing**—Each team must trace the patterns of their feet and cut them out. The group then puts all the feet together to form a picture. The other teams try to guess what the picture is displaying.

❸ **Feet Signing**—Everyone takes off shoes and socks. The group has two minutes to see how many signatures they get on their feet.

Following these or other games, move into a time of Bible study. Focus on Romans 10:12-15. Talk about verse 15 and the significance of beautiful feet. Discuss walking with Christ daily and being His servant. You may choose to close with a foot-washing ceremony.

Cardboard Camp-out

To sensitize youth to the feelings of the homeless, organize a "cardboard camp-out" in the church parking lot. The youth meet on a Friday night. Each one is given an assortment of cardboard boxes, newspapers, and duct tape, with which they have to build a shelter for themselves. The group builds fires in metal trash barrels to keep warm, and on every hour, there is a devotional study on such topics as faith in action (from the book of James) or the parable of the sheep and the goats, from Matthew 25.

Cartoon Parables

Divide youth into small groups of three or four. Assign a parable to each group. Provide each group with a poster board and markers. Instruct each group to read their parable and then draw the story in cartoon form on the poster board. This is a captivating way to get youth into the Gospels. After a designated amount of time, ask each team to present their cartoon to the large group. Discuss each parable briefly. At the end of the session, hang the cartoons on a focal wall to be enjoyed by others who use the room.

Creative Creator

This Bible study and discussion is especially effective on a retreat or in a camp setting. However, it can be used in almost any outdoor setting (such as a park near the church).

Begin by giving each youth a piece of blank paper and a pencil. Instruct them to walk and look around and to list all the things they notice about nature. Ask them to notice the colors, textures, sounds, smells. Tell them to pay attention to details.

After an ample amount of time, return to a large group. Ask the group for insights from their experience. After some discussion, ask the group what amazes them most about creation.

Use this question to lead into the actual study of the Bible and what Scripture has to say about the God who created it all. Scripture which may be used: Romans 1:19-20; Romans 8:18-25; Hebrews 11:3; Psalm 8:3-9; Genesis 1; Genesis 2:7.

Ask the group for the things they know about God after observing His creation and reading these Scriptures. Ask youth to share ways God speaks to them through His creation. Come up with additional questions which would be appropriate for your group.

Creative Worship

Instead of a regular Bible study time, ask youth to plan and lead a creative worship experience. Ahead of time decide on a theme for the worship experience and enlist youth to plan the order of worship; they will respond with surprising creativity. Divide youth into small groups and instruct each groups to be responsible for one of the different aspects of worship. For example, one group will lead music or provide special music. This does not mean someone has to sing a solo. They may choose to play a specific song for the large group off a CD or cassette. Another group can be responsible for presenting Scripture, drama, creative movement, or other forms of worship. At another time, discuss the elements of worship and ways one can worship God daily.

Crosswalk

This is a concept which works great for a group on a beach retreat. Try to find a stretch of undeveloped beach, without a whole lot of other people around. Make a large-sized cross out of wood—light enough for someone to be able to drag through the sand for a distance, but heavy enough for the person to have to struggle with it a bit. If you have a large group, you may want to have more than one cross. Each youth will also need to have a luminaria—a lighted candle in a paper bag, weighted with sand.

The idea of the Crosswalk is to present the seven sayings of Christ from the cross. The group begins walking down the beach, with one person carrying the cross, and everyone else carrying their luminarias. As he or she feels led, each person will silently take a turn at carrying the cross. Each will put down and leave the luminaria in the sand and then silently take the cross from the person carrying it. Every five minutes or so, stop and present one of the seven sayings. By the end of the walk, everyone will have taken a turn at carrying the cross. It is a powerful image to then turn and see the trail of light behind you. You can make a nice spiritual application about God's word being a lamp to our feet, or Jesus being the light of the world who made a way for us. On the way back, each person picks up a luminaria. The walk works best if it is done in silence between the devotional stops.

Distribution of Talents

This Bible study was based on the parable of the talents in Matthew 25:14-28. Each youth was given a certain amount of money out of the youth budget—between ten and twenty dollars. They were given

three months to put that money to work. At the end of three months, they were required to return at least the initial amount. Some youth put the money into a bank account and returned the money with interest. One youth used the money to buy gas for a lawn mower, then brought the money he made from mowing lawns all summer back to the church. Another youth used her money to buy the ingredients for cookies and brownies, which she made and sold.

For Better or Worse

This idea works great with youth as you discuss love and marriage. Divide the boys from the girls, forming two groups. Ask each group to brainstorm and list what they expect from a mate after marriage. Tell the two groups to be specific. After both groups have finished their lists, discuss their expectations in the large group. Eliminate those ideas which are totally unreasonable. Then each group writes their expectations in the form of wedding vows. Pick names of one boy and one girl from a hat and have a mock wedding ceremony. During the ceremony the "bride" reads the vows the boys wrote, and the "groom" reads those the girls wrote. Decorate in advance with flowers, balloons, rice, or even a wedding cake to enjoy after the ceremony. This event can lead into a Bible study on husband and wife roles in marriage or another related Bible study.

Easter Collage

During the Easter season involve youth in a Bible character study of the crucifixion, using Luke 23 as the study guide. Ask youth to create a giant collage of the crucifixion story. For several weeks choose a different passage of Scripture from Luke 23. Ask youth to read the passage, then choose key verses which give insight into the life of one of the persons associated with the crucifixion.

Distribute magazines, old posters, and other materials with plenty of photos. Instruct youth to find pictures which portray the attitudes and feelings of the person as revealed in the passage. Keep the pictures for each Bible person separate on the giant collage. Write the key verses under the picture cluster. When complete, the collage tells the Easter story in pictures. Display the collage on a prominent focal wall in the church for other members to see. Suggested characters and key verses are: the crowd, verse 21; Pilate, verse 24; Simon, verse 26; Jesus, verse 34; mockers, verses 35-37; Criminal One, verse 39; Criminal Two, verses 40-43; centurion, verse 47; Joseph, verse 50-53.

Get a Job

This works best if used as a series of Bible studies and events. Begin by studying various jobs and occupations in the Bible. Possible occupations and Scriptures may include:

- ✖ Advocate (lawyer)—1 John 2:1; John 14:16; 15:26; 16:7.
- ✖ Ambassadors—1 Kings 5:1; Isaiah 39:2; Numbers 20:14; Joshua 9:4-6; Judges 11:12; Ephesians 6:20; 2 Corinthians 5:20.
- ✖ Athlete—1 Corinthians 9:24-27; Acts 20:24; Romans 9:16; Galatians 2:2; Ephesians 6:12; 2 Timothy 4:7; 2 Timothy 2:5; Philippians 3:12-14; 1 Thessalonians 2:19; Hebrews 10:32-33.
- ✖ Centurion (soldier)—Genesis 40:3-4; 2 Kings 11:4-11; 1 Kings 22:33-34; Luke 7:1-10; Mark 15:39.
- ✖ Fisherman—Job 41:7; Isaiah 19:8; Matthew 13:47-48; Mark 1:16; Luke 5:2; Matthew 4:18-22.
- ✖ Musician—Matthew 9:23; Genesis 4:21; 1 Samuel 16:14-23.
- ✖ Overseer—Genesis 39:4-5; 2 Chronicles 2:8;

Nehemiah 11:9; Exodus 1:11-14; Acts 20:28; Philippians 1:1; 1 Timothy 3:2; Titus 1:7.
- ✖ Priest—Job 1:5; Numbers 8:9-18; Hebrews 2:9-14; Hebrews 9:28.
- ✖ Shepherd—Genesis 4:2; Genesis 13:7; 26:20; 30:36; Jeremiah 23:1-4; John 10:1-5; Psalm 23:2; Jeremiah 31:10; Ezekiel 34:12; Luke 15:4-5; Isaiah 40:11; 1Samuel 17:34-37; Amos 3:12; John 10:11.

Invite a variety of persons from within your own congregation to come and talk about their occupations with the youth group. Ask the individuals to share how they came to do that work and how being a Christian makes a difference on the job. Additional sessions may include career testing, tips for a professional interview, statistics on current job needs in various geographic areas, and other topics which would help youth in the job search. These sessions may be offered as a special focus for high school juniors and seniors or for those already in college trying to decide on a major study.

Gospel Truths and Doctor Seuss

In this series, the group used children's stories to make spiritual applications. There are a lot of really good such stories to be found in such Seuss classics as *Horton Hears a Who, The Butter Battle Book, Oh! The Places You'll Go!, The Lorax,* and others. Other excellent children's books that could be used in a series like this are *Alexander and the Terrible, Horrible, No Good, Very Bad Day* by Judith Viorst; *The Giving Tree, The Missing Piece,* and *The Missing Piece Meets the Big O* by Shel Silverstein; *The Rainbow Fish* by Marcus Pfister; and *The Velveteen Rabbit* by Margery Williams.

Grab Bag

Before the Bible study, select several verses of Scripture related to the topic you would like to discuss. Write down each verse on an index card and place the cards in a paper bag. During the session, ask volunteers to pull a card from the grab bag and read the verse to the large group. Ask volunteers to share what the verse means to them. Discuss ways they have or have not put this verse into practice during the last week. Explain the meaning of the verses in their context, relating biblical background and other information. Discuss how the Scriptures are relevant to us today.

Hands of Jesus

Divide youth into small groups. Instruct youth to look through the New Testament and find as many passages as possible where Jesus used His hands to help others. Ask the small groups to share their passages with the large group. Discuss each passage. Lead youth into a discussion of the way Christians today use their hands to reach others for Christ. Discuss ways of serving those in need.

Held in Bondage

In advance, make arrangements to visit your city police department, county sheriff's office, or a local juvenile detention center. Have the youth locked in jail for one hour or more. Discuss the Book of Philippians with your youth after the time limit. Discuss how Paul found joy even while he was in prison. Relate this to the many ways in which we are held in bondage. Discuss various topics such as freedom, bondage to sin, finding joy in difficult situations, and so forth.

How Did Jesus Feel?

The purpose of this Bible study is to help youth realize the humanness of Jesus. Youth will focus on the emotions Jesus felt during His earthly life. Begin by discussing how we all have emotions and how normal and essential they are as a part of life. Ask youth to think of different emotions they may have experienced during the past week. Instruct youth to think of situations at home, school, and church. Ask youth to remember different feelings they have experienced because of people in their lives. Ask them to write down their answers.

Tell youth to think of Jesus and His life as we know it through the Bible. Ask them to write down a separate list of emotions they believe Jesus experienced. Ask youth to share their answers in the large group. Write the list of emotions on a poster board and place it on a focal wall. Divide youth into small groups. Give each group one or two of the emotions listed on the poster board. Ask each small group to find at least one example in the Bible where Jesus might have felt that specific emotion. Look at the ways in which Jesus expressed His emotions. He seemed to always be honest and share His emotions in ways that helped others instead of hurting them. Discuss ways youth can express their emotions that help rather than hurt.

Human Slide Show

Divide your large group into small groups of no more than five. Give each small group a passage of Scripture. Each group is to pretend they are presenting a slide show presentation of the passage. The passage is divided into different "slides" to illustrate the story. The members of the groups position themselves into a still life pose to demonstrate each scene. One person from each group reads the passage of Scripture aloud, and the group poses in each "slide" at the appropriate time. The human slide show is a great way to depict and read the Scripture. Parables work especially well with this method of presenting Scripture.

Labels

Before the session write on index cards various titles or descriptions of people, using specific names if you want to. General types might include: a famous athlete, a homeless person, a movie star, a handicapped person, a person with cancer, or a person representing a different ethnic group and culture. As youth arrive, tape a card to each person's back, then direct them to mingle around the room, explaining that they should relate to another youth as they would to the person named on the other youth's card. But they are not to tell

the other what the card says. Allow plenty of time to interact, then form a large group. Discuss the way youth reacted to one another. Discuss any labels or prejudiced remarks, spoken or thought. Discuss how we are all equal in God's eyes. Possible Scripture might include Revelation 7:9 or Romans 3:22-23.

Light and Darkness

Begin this Bible study in the dark with only one candle lit or one small flashlight on. Give each person a flashlight (turned off) or an unlit candle. Discuss the ways the darkness hides things and makes it difficult to see. Ask youth to try to distinguish the colors of peoples' clothing or eyes. Allow youth to share their insights on darkness. Read various Scriptures relating to light and darkness, such as Genesis 1:3-4; John 8:12; 1 John 1:6. As a different passage is read, designate someone to turn on his flashlight or light her candle. As this continues, discuss how much easier it is to see things in the light. Stress that the light reflects the colors, making them more brilliant. Close by reading Matthew 5:14-16. Explain that we are never to hide our light as Christians. We are to provide what people need to see Christ clearly.

May-to-June Family Relationships Series

Each week between Mother's Day and Father's Day, focus on a different family role—mother, father, son, daughter, oldest, youngest, and so forth

Missionary Journeys

The missionary journeys of Paul work well with this Bible study. However, you may incorporate the journeys of a missionary in history or of one whom your church sponsors into the Bible study. This is great if you can go to a local park or to a retreat setting with a lake or pond.

Before youth arrive, set everything up. Use a map of the missionary journeys of Paul (or those of someone else) and lay everything

out. Put up signs to mark the locations of towns, cities, or countries. Label buildings or landmarks with signs or props.

When the group arrives, explain that they are about to go on a journey. As you progress through the cities and countries, stop at each one and read Scripture. Tell what Paul (or your missionary) did at that site or what happened there. You may have other adult leaders role play scenes at some of the stops. Use various modes of travel where appropriate (walk, boats or canoes, for example).

Music Search

Music is a powerful and permanent influence in teenagers' lives. Unfortunately, a lot of today's music has very negative messages. If you ask most youth, though, they will say "Oh, I never listen to the words; I just like the music." One youth minister created a Bible study called "Music Meltdown." She invited her youth to bring in their favorite secular music, along with the lyric sheet from the CD. The group looked at the words together, and discussed the potential harm in the lyrics. But this youth minister also built a sizable library of Christian music which provided alternatives to the secular music. In virtually every case, the minister could match a secular style with a Christian alternative. There are many music subscription services available to youth leaders which can help you build a music library.

Nail It to the Cross

In a Bible study or worship time about sin, give each student a piece of paper and a pencil. Invite them to write sins they are struggling with, and during an invitation time, to nail those sins to the cross.

Object Lesson Challenge

Each week, the youth minister challenged the group to bring him an object that he would <u>not</u> be able to use in making a spiritual application during a Bible study. If more than one object came in, the youth voted on which one they wanted to see him try. The next week, the youth minister presented the Bible study based on the item. The youth had a great time with it, and attendance increased each week as youth came back to see what the youth minister came up with. In a variation on this idea, the youth minister gave small groups each an object— for example, a watch, a roll of toilet paper, a coffee maker, and let them come up with spiritual applications. This was an excellent lead-in to a study on how Jesus used parables. It would also make a wonderful training session for VBS workers or youth teaching Backyard Bible Clubs on a mission trip.

One-Year Bible Discipleship Class

In December, invite youth to commit to reading the Bible through the next year. Provide copies of *The One Year Bible*, *The Daily Walk Bible*, or a similarly formatted Bible for each student. Once a week, prepare a group study on a key passage from that week.

On-Site Series

The idea is to take Bible study on location. Here are some ideas that have worked:

- ✖ A cemetery or funeral home to discuss death (or the resurrection).
- ✖ A maternity ward to talk about the gift of life.
- ✖ A junkyard for a discussion on materialism.
- ✖ A farm for the parable of the soil.
- ✖ The side of a highway for the good Samaritan.
- ✖ A lake or beach front for a study on John 21.

A spin-off of the On-Site concept would be to follow the entire life cycle over a period of time. Begin at a hospital, go to a baptism, a wedding (try to find one at a really big church where you can just be a spectator). Go on to a nursing home, a funeral, and a cemetery.

It might be interesting to arrange trips to other churches, and see how other denominations practice their faith. You might consider going to a Catholic christening or confirmation service, or to a Jewish Bar Mitzvah.

Parents of Teens Bible Study

A youth minister developed a Sunday School class for the parents of youth. Often parents and teens would discuss the same topics in their separate classes.

Paul's Letter to the Americans

Point out the letters written by Paul in the New Testament. Divide youth into several groups. Assign each group a different letter to use as a model. Ask youth to then rewrite the letter. Explain that youth are to write the letter as if Paul were writing it to Americans today. Instruct youth to include both positive and negative statements. At the end of the session, close by evaluating which of those things the youth group is or is not doing.

Phobia Studies

This is not really a study of phobias, but rather Bible studies with "twisted titles." Keep the subject matter secret. Build interest in the Bible studies by using phobia-related titles for the sessions. These titles are especially helpful to disguise serious topics which need to be addressed. Most youth don't really have these phobias, but they are hesitant to talk about the subjects. Twisted titles might include: "theophobia" when a session is about God; "jobaphobia" about work or finding a job; "jellophobia" discussing jealousy and envy; "flopophobia" would be fear of being a failure. The "phobia" series could be a special focus for a week or a month.

Question Box

A youth minister printed cards with "What does God say about..." at the top. Youth were invited to fill out the rest of each card with a question they had about the Bible. The youth minister answered a question each week in his newsletter column.

Questions, Comments, and Inspirations

This is a great Bible study idea which can be adjusted to fit the amount of time available for that session. Ask the group to read a specific passage of Scripture. Instruct the youth to write down at least one question, one comment, and one inspirational thought they have after reading the passage. After ample time, ask youth to divide into small groups to discuss their comments and inspirations. This is a great way for youth to learn from one another and have some of their questions answered. Return to a large group and discuss any questions still remaining after the share time. The leaders will need to be prepared to possibly facilitate the small groups and help youth keep their answers biblically based.

Step into the Future

The purpose of this Bible study is to help youth realize how their future is related to the decisions and choices they make now. Decorate the room with a space theme (*Star Trek*, for example) or a futuristic look. You can do this many ways. One way is to decorate with a lot of foil, silver wrapping paper, and mirrors.

As youth arrive, divide them into small groups of three or four. Give each group a sheet of poster board and markers. Ask youth to brainstorm these questions:

❶ What do you think the world will be like in ten years?

2 What are the main qualities or characteristics you think people will need to deal with the problems of the world in ten years? **3** What does the church need to do to help people prepare for the world in ten years? **4** What do you want your life to be like in ten years?

Ask the small groups to share their answers with the large group. Allow plenty of time for discussion. Focus on ways youth are preparing themselves spiritually for the future. Ask if they are taking advantage of all the opportunities available to them. Possible Scripture passages to incorporate: Matthew 6:33; Proverbs 3:5-6; 1 Peter 5:8.

Time Machine
Build a "time machine" with lights and plenty of sound. Each week have a different person dressed in character come out of the "time machine." Instruct youth to ask questions from a prepared worksheet. The time machine character will then answer or act out the answers to the questions and tell his or her story to the large group. It is a great way to make Old and New Testament personalities come to life.

Unexpected Visitor
One morning, a Sunday School teacher at one church dressed as a homeless man. He sat outside the entrance to the church with a sign saying, "Will Work For Food." Many of the youth passed him by on their way inside. Once inside, they talked about him to each other, with no clue that he was their Sunday School teacher. The youth got really nervous a few minutes later, when they saw him again, walking up and down the halls of the church. None of them recognized him as their Sunday School teacher until he came in to the room and removed part of the disguise. By that time, he definitely had their attention for a study on James 2 !

Using Crutches

For this Bible study enlist several youth to help role-play various Scripture passages which are about the lame people whom Jesus healed. Suggested passages of Scripture include: Mark 2:1-12; Matthew 9:1-8; John 5:1-15. After the role plays, discuss the characters presented. Lead the discussion on the importance of realizing that we are all handicapped without Christ.

❶ Ask youth for examples of "crutches" we use in place of Jesus at times in our lives.

❷ Discuss the ways in which sin cripples us from living an abundant life for Christ.

❸ Point out that it is only when we admit our handicaps (failings) that we learn to walk in the power of the Holy Spirit.

❹ Close by having youth lay their symbolic crutches at the foot of the cross. Lead in a time of prayer and commitment.

Why Christianity?

These questions and discussion starters are great for testing your youth's knowledge of the basics. Many of the questions are deliberately antagonistic towards Christianity. However, youth need to have answers for those types of people in the world. You can use several of the questions at one session or only one. These questions could enhance a doctrinal study at your church and/or help encourage youth to participate in witnessing training.

❶ "If God is so loving, why does He allow so much pain and suffering in the world?"

❷ "Why do you believe in God? Don't use the Bible as proof, because I don't believe the Bible is true."

❸ "How can you prove that prayer really works? What evidence do you have of the power of prayer?"

❹ "What is so special about the Bible? Why do you believe it?"

❺ "How do you know Jesus Christ is who He said He was?"

❻ "How do you know Christ is alive today?"

7 "How can Christians believe in the resurrection of Jesus? What proof is there to support this belief?"

8 "Most people that go to church and claim to be Christians are hypocrites. Why would anyone want to be a Christian?"

9 "How do we know the right books are in the Bible?"

10 "You always hear Christians talk about having a personal relationship with Jesus Christ. What is the big deal?"

Add Your Own Ideas Here:

_____

_____

_____

_____

_____

_____

_____

_____

_____

_____

Games and Fellowships

One of the job requirements for youth ministry is a certain measure of kookiness. A little goofiness goes a long way in bringing your youth together, breaking down walls between group members, and creating an atmosphere of energy, enthusiasm, and expectancy. These are key conditions for spiritual development. Never underestimate the power of fun and the need for goofiness in your ministry. If you are not, by nature, a kook, pray that God will send a good measure of kooks your way. Here are some ideas to get your creative juices flowing. Not to mention orange juices, apple juices, chocolate syrup, Jello...

All Tied Up
Everyone wears a tie to the Sunday evening service, and at the after-church fellowship have prizes for widest, wildest, ugliest, and so forth. All the games can involve being tied: Twister, three-legged races, amoeba volleyball (see "Night of a Thousand Volleyballs"). A devotional could be given on being bound together in Christ or how God frees us from bondage.

Here are two bonus ideas for All Tied Up:

❶ **It's Knot Easy:** Form groups of five to eight. Each group makes a circle, and each person in the circle grabs the hands of two <u>different</u> people across the circle. No one can grab hands with the person to their

immediate left or right. Then the group tries to get untangled without breaking hands.

❷ **Tube-a-Ruba:** You can do this either as individuals or in small groups of three or four. Purchase several feet of wide-diameter clear flexible tubing from a hardware store or pet supply store. Wrap the tubing around the group or individual. Put a marble in one end. The group (or individual) twists and turns and gyrates until the marble comes out the other end.

Annual Birthday Party

Decorate a large room for a giant birthday party. Arrange twelve tables and decorate each table according to the month it represents. Prepare a birthday cake for each table or one giant cake representing the twelve months. Plan games and provide party favors. Invite each person to bring a gift which could be given to either a male or female. As guests arrive they are to sit at the table corresponding to their birthday month. Gifts may be traded at the tables or each gift may be tagged with a number. Later in the party, each person may draw a number and receive their gift. You may choose to recognize the oldest, the youngest, the person with a holiday birthday, February 29 birthdays, and so forth.

Apathy Party

This was a good "attitude check" fellowship for one church. Every person is handed a grocery bag when he or she comes through the door. The rules for the fellowship—no laughing, no enthusiasm, no expression of any emotion whatsoever. If, at any time, a youth loses control and acts like she's excited about something, she has to put the bag over her head until she regains her "coolness." Fill the evening with so many crazy activities that youth can't help but laugh and have a good time. Conclude the evening with a devotion about apathetic attitudes.

Baby Contest

Ask youth to bring a picture of themselves when they were one year old or younger. The photo needs to be a single photo with no one else pictured. Youth are to keep their photo hidden from others in the group, but they need to write their name on the back. Number each photo and place them on a focal wall. Everyone is to number a piece of paper according to the numbers on the wall and decide who each baby is. The group will also vote on: most likely to cry, most likely to bite, most likely to break new toys, most likely to spit up, bad hair day baby, good hair day baby, and so forth. This is a great activity to begin a Bible study on Psalm 139, "You Are Wonderfully Made."

Bad Hair Day

This fellowship focuses on hair activities. Begin with a bad hair day contest. Divide into teams and give each team a can of shaving cream. One volunteer from each team will have his or her hair arranged into a "bad hair-do" using shaving cream. After the teams have completed the bad hair-do, the large group votes on the worst hair.

   Another game requires another volunteer from each team. This time clear packing tape is wrapped around their head. (Sticky side out!) Each team is then given several hundred Q-Tips swabs and cotton balls. The "tape head" sits in the middle of the circle with team members forming the outer circle. At the signal, team members begin throwing the Q-Tips and cotton balls, trying to make them stick to the tape. Caution them about possible injuries to eyes from the Q-Tips. After two minutes call for the groups to stop. Again, have the large group vote on the tape heads in several categories. They may vote on best hair, worst hair, most hair (remem-

bering that "hair" in this case is the cotton balls and Q-Tips).

These are just two games to get the group started. Other games may include using wigs, silly string, mops, and so forth. Be creative.

Bedroom of the Week

Though not really a fellowship, this became a fun part of the regular Wednesday night Bible study. Each week, a student's bedroom is videotaped while he or she is at school. No one knows until they watch the video who gets the "Bedroom of the Week" award.

Bible Clues

This is a treasure hunt using clues from the Bible. Choose verses in the Bible that contain words which can point youth to specific

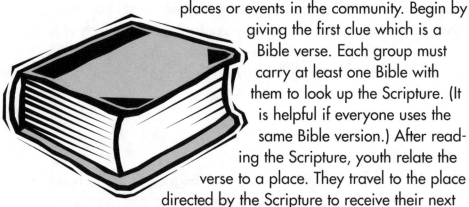

places or events in the community. Begin by giving the first clue which is a Bible verse. Each group must carry at least one Bible with them to look up the Scripture. (It is helpful if everyone uses the same Bible version.) After reading the Scripture, youth relate the verse to a place. They travel to the place directed by the Scripture to receive their next clue (Scripture). Each clue will lead youth closer to the treasure. Be sure to give each group different clues if possible so one group does not just follow another group. It is best to use at least five clues for each group, and try to space the clues the same distance for each group so traveling times will be equal. The treasure can be anything, but make sure it was worth the hunt. It works great to have the treasure be an ice cream fellowship with friends at the end of a hot summer evening!

Some possible verses which could be used as clues are: Psalm 23:2, green pasture or water; Psalm 119:105, lamp or light; John 4:6, well; Proverbs 26:14, door; Proverbs 26:20, wood or fire; Proverbs 7:20, purse, money (bank). Map out the places youth will go to get the clues, then use your Bible concordance to help with the Scripture clues.

Broomball

Rent an ice skating rink and play hockey, using brooms and a volleyball.

Bumper Boxes

For this activity you will need a refrigerator box for each team. Ask each team to decorate their box and select a team name. One player from each team gets inside the box, standing up, with the box over his or her head. This person may also be blindfolded to make sure all play fair. The open end of the box is down on the floor so the person can walk. On the signal, the players "race" to the goal or opposite wall and back. The individual in the box must receive all his or her directions from teammates. The teammates must yell the directions from behind the starting line. Since the players cannot see, they run into each other, go the wrong way, and other crazy things. Because of the possibility of injury, prohibit running—it will be funny enough when they walk!

Candle Guard/Fizz Tag with Water Guns

These are both great water gun games. In Candle Guard, each person has a lit candle; they are trying to keep theirs lit while at the same time trying to shoot everyone else's lights out. This game can lead to some effective debriefing about being the light of the world, and about the things which threaten to extinguish your light.

In Fizz Tag, drill holes through the center of Alka-Seltzer tablets so they can be worn around the neck. The last person to have any part of the Alka-Seltzer still intact wins. It is not fair to hold the Alka-Seltzer in your hand.

5
1

Chicken Night

Here is an example of a <u>theme</u> fellowship. All the songs, games and activities deal with chickens. There are egg tosses, games with feathers, and a relay which involves putting together a chicken out of a bag of fryer parts and a roll of masking tape. (Each of the bags has one or two extra parts; that makes for some interesting finished products). You could modify the Turkey Bowl idea as part of this fellowship (see Turkey Bowl 2.) Just make sure you don't step over the "fowl" line! For a snack the group had chicken fajitas.

Chop Fooey

Secure enough chopsticks for each participant to have a pair. Divide the group into several teams. Explain that each person on the the team will be given chopsticks, and the team will have one bowl of food to pass from player to player. As a team they will work together to try to eat their bowl of food the fastest. However, every person on the team must take at least <u>one</u> bite of the food. The bowls may contain any food from Jello or pudding to peas or corn. The first team to finish wins!

Clothes Pins

This is a great game to play with any size group. Give everyone five to ten clothespins. Make sure everyone has the same number. On "go," each person tries to pin his or her clothespins to the other players' clothing (not skin!). Each clothespin must be hung on a different person. Of course, each player must keep moving to avoid having clothespins hung on him or her. At the end of the time limit the person with the fewest clothespins is the winner.

Clue—More or Less

This one takes a lot of advance preparation, but it is worth it! It

works well in a camp or retreat setting, where there are a few faculty and a large number of adult volunteers.

The basic idea is for small groups to solve a mystery. First assign to faculty or staff members the roles of most of the various characters (similar to those from the board game CLUE®)—Colonel Catsup, Miss Crimson, Professor Pear, Mrs. Black, and Mrs. Partridge. An object turns up missing at Mrs. Black's dinner party, for example, a pet hamster. An opening skit establishes each character's motive for stealing the hamster, how it could have been done, and what Sinister Plan that character might have had in mind. If possible, shoot a video beforehand to set up the game, showing all the possible methods of escape and Sinister Plans. Then shoot another video which solves the mystery to show when all groups return.

Small groups are responsible for figuring out who stole the hamster, how the hamster was taken from the dinner party, and what sinister plan had been in store for the rodent.

Small groups are then sent to various locations on the campus, where they can perform different stunts in order to get clues to solve the mystery. An adult counselor is stationed at each location to verify the stunt and give out the clue.

In addition, the five characters are located in various places on campus as well. Groups are allowed to ask them each one question which can be answered yes or no (they cannot ask if the person stole the hamster). All the clues point to one character, one method of escape, and one Sinister Plan, so that by logic and the process of elimination, the mystery can be solved. When a group thinks they have the mystery solved, they return their Detective Sheet to a timekeeper, who writes down their time at the top of their sheet.

The following pages are provided to help you develop the game for your group. These can be used as they are or modified to fit your group. Each group will need one Detective Sheet in solving the mystery. Another page lists stunts which may be used for the group to earn clues. And, of course, there is a list of clues included. This game usually takes a full hour of time to complete. It is fun for everyone.

Detective Sheet

Where Is Piglet?

Suspects:

	YES	NO
Colonel Catsup (C.C.)	❏	❏
Professor Pear (P.P.)	❏	❏
Miss Crimson (M.C.)	❏	❏
Mrs. Black (M.B.)	❏	❏
Mrs. Partridge (M.P.)	❏	❏

Method:

	C.C.	P.P.	M.C.	M.B.	M.P.
Guitar case	❏	❏	❏	❏	❏
Pregnant disguise	❏	❏	❏	❏	❏
Picnic cooler	❏	❏	❏	❏	❏
Backpack	❏	❏	❏	❏	❏
Oil can	❏	❏	❏	❏	❏
Hid in a hat	❏	❏	❏	❏	❏

Evil Plan:

	C.C.	P.P.	M.C.	M.B.	M.P.
Throw off cliff	❏	❏	❏	❏	❏
Set adrift in lake	❏	❏	❏	❏	❏
Use by person to bowl	❏	❏	❏	❏	❏
Play Piglet Putt-Putt	❏	❏	❏	❏	❏
Let loose on freeway	❏	❏	❏	❏	❏
Fluff in the dryer	❏	❏	❏	❏	❏

Stunts

❶ As a group, sing "Row, Row, Row Your Boat" backwards. Turning around and facing the wall does not count!

❷ Perform a lap sit. Group gets into a tight, shoulder-to-shoulder circle, turns their left shoulder in, then sits down together. They should be in a tight enough circle so that when they sit down, they are on each others' laps. They must then sing one verse of "Old McDonald Had a Farm."

❸ The group must line up in the order of their birthdays.

❹ Name three things about the local town.

❺ The group must line up tallest to shortest.

❻ Make a list of ten things you love about Piglet.

❼ The group must build a pyramid, no more than four high.

❽ As a group, perform twenty jumping jacks.

❾ Name ten characters from the *Peanuts* comic strip.

❿ Spell out "Piglet" with your bodies.

⓫ As a group, sing the "Beaver" song, only substitute "Piglet" for "Beaver."

⓬ As a group, recite the alphabet from Z to A.

⓭ Give your adult leader a big group hug. Tell him or her you love them three times.

⓮ As a group, name ten different candy bars.

⓯ Line up your group alphabetically by last names.

5
5

Clues

Adults: Do not show this sheet to the players. Remember, the groups can ask you for only **ONE** clue. They have to ask for the clues by number. If they ask for one they already have, too bad!

❶ Professor Pear loves mountain cliffs.

❷ Colonel Catsup does his laundry every week.

❸ Professor Pear and Miss Crimson would never go bowling.

❹ The kidnapper has hairy legs.

❺ Mrs. Black is the only one who plays guitar.

❻ The kidnapper is from the South.

❼ Piglet was not kidnapped by Professor Pear.

❽ The evil plan does not involve setting Piglet adrift in the lake.

❾ Mrs. Partridge loves to go on picnics, but nobody else does.

❿ Mrs. Black and Miss Crimson were seen last week at the putt-putt course. Colonel Catsup was not with them.

⓫ Neither Colonel Catsup nor Professor Pear would ever go near the freeway.

⓬ Only Miss Crimson and Mrs. Black own backpacks.

⓭ Only Mrs. Partridge owns a big hat.

⓮ None of the women used the pregnant disguise.

⓯ Piglet was not taken out in the oil can.

Here are the rules:

❶ When you get your Detective Sheet, write your group's name at the top of it.

❷ You must hold hands with your group at all times.

❸ Each suspect will be in a different room in the building. You may ask each of the suspects one question, which can be answered "yes" or "no." (You cannot ask—in any form—if he/she is the guilty one.) You may go back and ask the suspect a second question, but only after you have gone to all of the suspects once. The suspects will initial your Detective Sheet each time.

❹ You may get additional clues by completing different tasks as a group. After you complete the task, ask the adult at that station for a numbered clue (1-15). Keep track of which clues you have asked.

❺ When you think you have solved the mystery, come back to the auditorium. An adult on stage will take your card and write down the time you checked in.

Coffee House

A great fellowship night at camp or anytime is to have a coffee house program. Divide youth into small groups and ask them to come up with coffee house entertainment.

This may be singing, drama, poetry reading, comedy, and so forth. During the evening each group will have the opportunity to present their entertainment for the large group. Set up small tables and chairs in groups of no more than six. Use candles on the tables for light. Provide coffee, hot chocolate, popcorn, cookies, donuts, or similar items for the refreshments. Provide music as youth arrive. This can be a crazy, fun time, or it may be more serious. You may even want to close the evening with a time of prayer or sharing.

Commercial Quiz

Ask youth to sit in a circle and give one person a water gun. Ask the person with the water gun to complete part of the slogan or identify the product advertised in the commercial. You have the list of commercial quotes. You read only a part of the commercial. If the player knows the answer, he or she gets to squirt another person sitting in the circle. If he or she does not know the answer, the water gun is passed on to the next person in the circle. Then read part of another commercial quote.

Corn Shucking Race

Divide youth into groups of six. Each team member must lie in a circle on his or her back with feet in the air, meeting in the center of the circle. A piece of corn is then placed on the elevated feet. The object is for team members to shuck the corn. Then

another piece of corn is placed on their feet and so on until a three minute time limit is up. The team who has shucked the most corn wins.

CRASH Night
An outreach fellowship. CRASH stands for "Christians Running Around Snatching Humans." Youth are sent out to bring back as many of their friends as possible for a combination fellowship and Bible study.

Drive-In Movie
If you have a video projector, you can turn your church parking lot into a drive-in by sewing several sheets together and hanging them on the side of your church. This could be an effective fund-raiser as well if youth take orders for burgers, hot dogs, fries and malts from each car. They could even be on roller skates. Watch a horrible, '50's-drive-in-type movie, like *Godzilla* or *Planet of the Apes*. One youth minister who had access to a high school football field adapted this idea by hanging a large sheet between the goal posts.

Note: Remember that you will need to get a license to show a movie publicly.

Fifth Quarter Fellowships
These are held after home games at the high schools. Have youth workers with video cameras at the games, getting shots of your youth who are on the football team, in the band, cheerleaders, drill

team, or in the stands. Show the videos at the fellowship.

> **Note:** If you have several high schools represented in your youth group, do your best to find nights when all of them are in town. Or have several different Fifth Quarters throughout the season. The perception of bias toward one school can be damaging to a ministry.

'Fifties Night

Rent a local diner, play '50's music, lip-sync to '50's songs, and dress up. The youth minister presents a devotional on how times change, but God's love does not.

Fizz Relay

This is an excellent relay to do outside! Divide the group into teams. Provide enough Alka-Seltzer tablets for each person to have one. You will need a pitcher for each team and a water source (faucet or large water container) to fill their pitcher. Line up the teams relay style behind a start line. On the signal, the first person in line runs to the source and fills the pitcher with water. This person returns to the start line and begins pouring water into the cupped hands of the person next in line. This person has an Alka-Seltzer tablet in his or her cupped hands. When the tablet is completely dissolved, this person runs to fill the pitcher with water and then returns to begin filling the hands of the next person in line. The first team to completely dissolve all of their Alka-Seltzer tablets is the winner.

Foot Scrabble

Have ten to fifteen people on a team. The object is to have your team spell out words in a given category, using letters written on the soles of their feet with magic marker. Each team has a few minutes to write their letters on their feet. With older groups, you can let them pick the letters they want to write. With younger ones, its best to choose them yourself, making sure there is a fair mix of vowels and consonants.

Have a list of several categories, for example, a New Testament book, an Old Testament book, a U.S. city, a current movie. Read one to the group. Each team then must lie down with their feet lined up, soles out, spelling out their answer. It has to be readable, from left to right, from your perspective. Award one point to the team who gets a word spelled out first, and two points for the longest word spelled out. (That way, the group that spells out "JUDE" doesn't get as many points as the group that figures out "SECOND THESSALONIANS"). It is really a fun game— sort of a combination of "Wheel of Fortune" and "Twister." You can make an entire fellowship theme around feet. Maybe the devotion could be on Isaiah 52:7— "How beautiful are the feet of them that bring glad tidings."

Frisbee Tournament

This works great as an afternoon or all-day event. A flying disk (Frisbee) tournament is also a great way to involve unchurched youth. Encourage youth to bring their own Frisbees. But bring plenty of extra Frisbees for those who forget. Plan ahead and make the necessary arrangements to secure a large grassy area or section of a park. As youth arrive, ask them to sign up for various Frisbee events and games. Some of the games require team participation; give them time to think of team names and make team banners. Schedule the various events throughout the day. Make sure that youth are not so busy that they miss watching some of the events. Provide refreshments or have youth bring their own "brown bag." Possible Frisbee events include: Frisbee golf, Frisbee relays, an accuracy contest, distance contest, "fanciest" throw, trick catching, and so forth

Furniture Smash

Although this activity is a little violent, it really is fun. Divide youth into teams of four or five. Give each team a piece of furniture which has been donated or picked up from the city dump. Furniture needs to be fairly equal in size, for example, a chair, a table, a bookshelf. The idea is for each team to smash their piece of furni-

ture and then fit the entire thing into a small cardboard box and close the lid. It is a crazy idea but lots of fun.

Fruitful Fellowship

Another theme idea. All the songs, games, and events have to do with fruit. Sing songs about fruit (for example, *Fruits of the Spirit, I Like Bananas*). Play "fruity" games, serve banana splits, and conclude with a devotion on the fruits of the Spirit.

Going Ape

An ape theme fellowship, or lock-in. Serve banana bread and banana splits, have a Tarzan look-alike contest, and have an all-night marathon of *Planet of the Apes*-type* movies. (You will want to preview any movie you decide to use to make sure it is appropriate for your viewing audience.)

One fun ape game is Gorilla-Man-Gun which is sort of a full-body rock-paper-scissors game. Partners stand back-to-back and chant this together:

> "Gorilla beats the man.
> The man beats the gun.
> The gun beats the gorilla.
> If you tie, you die.
> One, Two, Three, Turn!"

Pairs turn and face each other, each giving one of the three signs (Gorilla— beats on chest; Man— holds hand out for handshake; Gun— points gun). If both have the same sign, both sit down. Otherwise, the winner pairs up with winner from another partnership for Round Two. Play until there is one winner.

Greased Youth Minister Chase

A Humane Society approved alternative to the greased pig chase. Several youth ministers in one area got together for this one. Greased head to toe with baby oil, they were chased around a pen by their youth until they were wrestled to the ground. A prize was given to the last youth minister standing. This could also be used with summer camp faculty, Sunday School teachers, deacons, ministerial staff....

Ha Ha Game

This is a great beginning game for any fellowship or activity. One person lies down on the floor on his or her back. The next person lies down at right angles to the first with his or her head on the first person's stomach. The third person lies down with his or her head on the second person's stomach and so on. After all are on the floor with their heads on someone's stomach, the first person says "ha." The second person then says "ha-ha," and the third person says "ha-ha-ha." This continues with each person saying the number of "ha's" depending on the number in the line up. Try to get the group to do this seriously. If anyone messes up make the group start over. It is good for lots of laughs, literally.

Hair-Raising Fellowship

Youth are divided into groups. Each group has hair dryers, curlers, mousse, gel, and industrial strength hair spray. Each group has about thirty minutes to interpret a passage of Scripture with a hairstyle. One person in each group is the model (or victim, depending on how you look at it). Scripture passages: Moses and the burning bush (Exodus 3), crossing the Red Sea (Exodus 14), the Tower of Babel (Genesis 11:1-9), the fiery furnace (Daniel 3), Jesus calming the storm (Mark 4:35-41), the walls of Jericho falling down (Joshua 6:1-21), or (if you're really brave) the story of Samson and Delilah (Judges 16). This one works well in a camp setting, where youth can get away to different rooms to prepare their creations (and where they will have access to a lot of different hair dryers and curlers).

Happy Goodyear

For your next New Year's Eve party, what about selecting a theme revolving around tires or cars. Divide youth into teams. Ask each team to come up with a name and a cheer. Then play some of these wild games or make up your own.

❶ **Through the Hoop:** Hang a tire from a tree by a rope. Teams race to see which can all dive through the tire in the fastest time. Time the event and award the winning team. Be sure something (such as a mattress) is prepared to give them a "soft landing."

❷ **Amoeba:** See how many youth can stand inside a large tractor tire tube. The tube needs to be waist high. Then have the "amoebas" race one another.

❸ **Tire Relay:** Roll tires with a person inside it. Race relay style.

❹ **Slalom:** Set up a slalom course. Ask the teams to roll the tires along the course all at the same time. It is wild.

❺ **Stack Up:** Teams compete to see which can stack a pile of tires the highest.

Hunt for Red October

A very large water-balloon fight with a theme. Youth are divided into teams of ten. Each team makes a refrigerator box into a "submarine." The sub must be big enough for five people (the crew) at

a time, and only the captain can see where it is going, because there is one "periscope hole" cut in the front of the box. Play on a large field. Each team has a base from which their sub is launched. At the base, there are the other five team members with a water balloon launcher and about a zillion water balloons. In the field are different objects (or adult sponsors) in Hula Hoops. The object is to collect objects and bring them back to the base. If a sub is hit five times with water balloons on the way to pick up an object or on the way back, they have to return the object to the hoop, go back to their base, switch sub crews, and wait two minutes for "repairs to be made." Water balloon launchers can be found at most toy stores.

Ice Fishing

Fill two pans with crushed ice and place several marbles in the bottom of the pans, underneath the ice. Two volunteers then remove their socks and shoes and race to see who can get the marbles out of the pan of ice the fastest, using only their toes! They are not allowed to turn the pan over or spill any ice. The winner is the first to get all the marbles.

International Progressive Dinner

This is the same concept as a traditional progressive dinner, but with a missions emphasis. Each location represents a different country. Have groups of students responsible for hosting each country. They research the country, its customs, clothing, and so forth, and try to make each house as authentic as possible. The youth minister wrote to missionaries in those countries and had the letters read at the appropriate houses. Afterwards, students regularly corresponded with those missionaries.

65

Junior/Senior Valentine Banquet

Use a Valentine banquet to kick off a year-long partnership between youth and senior adults. Pair them up, have them send birthday and Christmas cards to each other, and plan other activities throughout the year. Culminate with a picnic in the spring.

Kiddie Pool Kickball

Regular kickball rules apply, except that each base is an inflatable wading pool. Have hoses running to each one to keep the pools filled. If you play on grass, the slides are hilarious. Afterwards, don't be surprised if an impromptu mud wrestling tournament breaks out.

Long John Stuff

Select two or three youth and have each one put on a pair of long johns (size XXL) over their clothes. Give the large group balloons to blow up and tie off. You will probably need at least one hundred balloons. On a signal, two participants for each person in long johns begins stuffing the balloons into the long johns. The balloons should be stuffed in the legs, arms, and body of the long johns. The idea is to get the most balloons into the pair of long johns in a two minute period. At the end of the two minutes, the long john wearers count the balloons by popping them with a pin through the long johns.

Magazine Hunt

Divide into small groups. Give each group one magazine with plenty of pictures. Every group starts with their magazine closed. The leader then begins by saying "Find a picture of... (and names any object)," and each group races to find it. The first group to find the picture earns a certain number of points. The higher the points the more exciting the game seems to be. Occasionally during the game ask the groups to trade their magazine with another group.

Items to have the groups look for might include a watch, a street sign, a fish, a boat, an umbrella, and so forth.

Marshmallow Golf

Borrow some golf putters and plastic putting cups from members of your congregation or buy some from a local sporting goods store. Lay out a course around the church. In winter, you may possibly do this inside the church with permission. Use steps and set up other obstacles to make the course tougher and more interesting. Players tee up their marshmallow on its rounded side when starting, but once it has been hit it must be played where and as it is. This is a challenging game and always gets some laughs.

Monster Make-Up

Select several pairs for this event. Usually guys sit in chairs facing the large group. Then their partners "make up" their faces with various "cosmetics." The cosmetics are peanut butter, toothpaste, shaving cream, and other messy items. The large group then judges the monsters to determine the ugliest.

Mud Pies

This is an exciting event that most people only dream about (or have nightmares about!). Find a large area of land. Ask permission to dig it up and then add plenty of water to create a <u>big</u> area of mud. You might have to bring in some dirt to avoid some of the digging. The area needs to big enough to play games in, and the mud should be about one foot deep. Make sure youth wear clothes that can be thrown away after the event. During the mud games have a few hoses available to keep the mud nice and gooey. You can also use them to wash mud off the youth when necessary. Some suggested mud games:

> **Mud Sculpture:** Divide youth into teams. Ask each team to create a sculpture from the mud. Set a time limit. When time is up, judge the sculptures on most mud used, most recognizable form, nicest consistency of mud, and so forth.

Mud <u>Packing</u>: Divide into teams. Ask each team to completely cover (except for the head!) one member of
their team in mud. Time this event and see which
team does it the fastest.

Mud <u>Slinging</u>: This event can be very creative. The contests
should include throwing mud at each other or at a
target. Caution players to avoid opponents' eyes and
to be sure the mud thrown contains no rocks or other
hard material.

Mud <u>Ball</u>: This is played like football, with tackling in the
mud. Set a time limit on the game. The purpose is to
get very dirty, not to play a full length game.

Mud <u>Long</u> <u>Jump</u>: Form a single file line. Instruct youth to
run and jump for distance. Of course, they land in
the mud!

Mud <u>Pie</u> <u>Throwing</u> <u>Contest</u>: Ask the teams to make mud
pies using the mud and pie tins. On the signal, the
teams begin throwing the mud pies (not the tins).
There is no winner or loser, necessarily, unless you
judge by the amount of mud on each team member.
Good luck!

The list of games could go on and on. Be creative and have fun!

Music Video Fellowship

Enlist several volunteers who would be
willing to come and use their video
cameras for this event. Purchase
the necessary number of VHS
tapes for the cameras. Divide
youth into small groups and
give them several songs to
choose from for their music video.
It works great to use television theme songs
so the youth actually sing the words instead of lip syncing. Instruct

each group to meet in rooms separate from each other and from the large group to get their act together. After fifteen or twenty minutes, ask the camera operators to begin taping the music videos, going from room to room. Make sure none of the small groups watch each other taping or practicing. To keep things moving, tell the groups that they get only one "take." At the conclusion of the filming, have everyone meet together for snacks and show all the videos. It is great to see what the groups come up with, and the bloopers only add to the event.

Newspaper Costumes

Divide the group into small groups of three to five. Give each group 15 pieces of newspaper and 15 straight pins. The groups then design an original costume for one of their members in 15 minutes. The groups will be judged on creativity, neatness, originality, or any other categories agreed upon in advance. After the fifteen minutes, allow a panel of judges to evaluate the designs.

Night of a Thousand Volleyballs

Have an entire fellowship in which different variations of volleyball are played. For example:

❶ **Blind Volleyball:** Sheets and blankets are draped over the net so you cannot see where the ball is coming from.

❷ **Multi-Ball Volleyball**

❸ **Blanket Catch Volleyball:** Players in pairs catch the ball in a beach towel and toss it back across the net.

❹ **Cooperation Volleyball:** Start with everyone on one side, play until everyone is on the other side. You get

unlimited hits on each side, and whoever volleys the ball over runs to the other side. If the ball hits the ground, everybody goes back to one side.

❺ <u>**Elimination Volleyball:**</u> When you make a mistake, you are out. (Idea for debriefing: play Cooperation Volleyball and Elimination Volleyball one after the other. Talk about which one gave players a better feeling. Which one is more like the world? Which is more like your youth group?)

❻ <u>**Amoeba Volleyball:**</u> Tie groups of four together with lengths of rope—back-to-back-to-back-to-back. Regular volleyball rules apply.

❼ <u>**"100":**</u> A team gets one point for every time they bump the ball, but no one person can hit the ball twice in a row. If they send the ball over the net before it hits the ground on their side, they keep their accumulated points. But if the ball drops, they lose all the points they accumulated since the last time they had the ball. First side to reach 100 points wins.

❽ <u>**Four Square Volleyball:**</u> Two nets at right angles to each other divide the court into quadrants. Divide your group into four equal groups. Designate one square to be Number One, then Number Two, Three, and Four. The object is to work your way to the Number One square. If the team in one quadrant doesn't return the ball or sends it out of bounds, they have to go to the Number Four square, and everyone else moves up.

"P" Party

A fellowship in which everything starts with the letter "P." Hold a pool party with pizza and Pepsi (and Pringle's, of course). Everyone wears pink, purple, polka dots, plaid, or pajamas. The devotional can be on prayer.

Poster Puzzle

Divide the large group into teams. You will need as many posters as you have teams. Cut the posters into pieces, making jigsaw puzzle pieces. Keep out one piece from each poster; then mix all the rest of the pieces together in a large bag or box. Count out an even number of pieces to put in separate bags, one bag for each team. Begin play by giving each team one of the original puzzle pieces and assigning them to working on that poster. At the signal, each team will try to complete their poster to win. Eventually each team will realize that some of the pieces they need are in another team's bag. The teams can then trade pieces (one for one) to complete their puzzle posters. This is a great game to play as a motivational activity before doing a Bible study on working together as the body of Christ.

Prom Alternative

The prom can be a pretty negative thing, not just because of the alcohol, but because of what it can do to the self-esteem of youth who don't have a date. Many churches have had great success planning a blow-out fellowship on prom night.

Regressive Dinner

A new twist on a progressive dinner. Start with dessert. Of course, this opens up a host of other possibilities: an Aggressive Dinner, where you only have one food portion for all of your guests; a Digressive Dinner, where every time you start to have dinner you get distracted; or a Transgressive Dinner, where no one can eat because of sin in their lives.

Reindeer Hunt

This idea could be used any time during the Christmas holidays. Take the entire group to a shopping mall or another place where there are lots of people. Divide the large group into smaller teams of four or five. Give each team a list of Santa's reindeer. (Dasher, Dancer, Prancer, Vixen, Comet, Cupid, Donner, Blitzen, Rudolph.) Give clues beside each reindeer's name that helps to identify them. For example, "Dancer has red shoes." Enlist nine adult volunteers as the reindeer. Each reindeer has specific boundaries where he or she needs to remain during the game. The object is for each team to find all nine of the reindeer and get their autographs on a sheet of paper. The teams must go up to the individuals and ask them if they are a reindeer or call them by their reindeer names. Use adults whom the teams will not recognize immediately. It may be wise to get permission from the management before playing the game in their stores.

Scavenger Hunts

Scavenger hunts date back at least to the time God said to Noah, "Bring two of every kind of animal to the ark." Where would youth ministry be without the time-honored scavenger hunt? Here are some ideas which may be fresh to you.

✖ **Identity Check:** Pair up with another church youth group in town (maybe where most of the kids go to a different school than your kids go to). Arrange a few weeks ahead of time to do a school picture swap— you get pictures from all your kids, the other youth minister from his or her kids. Send the other youth minister the pictures, and vice versa. Then on the day of your event have your groups go to the mall at the same time, each group parking at opposite ends of the mall. Pass out the school pictures from the other church to your kids. The object of the game is for kids to find the kid from the other church whose picture they have. (Or, as a variation, photocopy all the pictures and put them on one sheet, then pass out the sheets). When everyone has been found, meet in the food court, then go back to one of the two churches

for a combined fellowship, then a Bible study on being one in Christ.

✖ <u>**Church**</u> <u>**Trivia**</u> <u>**Hunt:**</u> During a lock-in, have teams of youth find the number of pews in the sanctuary. Then have them find that number in the hymnal. They are to find out and write down who wrote it and when. Design additional instructions to fit your church.

✖ <u>**Airport**</u> <u>**Hunt:**</u> If you live near a large airport, conduct your scavenger hunt there. Possible items— an air sickness bag from Quantas Airlines, a pilot's auto- graph, the number of fire alarms in the trans- portation mall, the location of the tele- phone with a certain  number, the location of a certain painting or sculp- ture, and so forth. A great way to introduce your new Sunday School teachers for the year is to disguise them and hide them in a mall or airport.

✖ <u>**Wal-Mart**</u> <u>**Hunt:**</u> Each person receives a list of items with the price of each. The youth find each item and record its bar code to show that they have found it. They work in pairs, and the first to find every item is the winner. Put a lot of very obscure items on the list, and it will take a couple of hours to finish. This would work well in a lock-in. Make sure you contact Wal-Mart (or other discount store) to get permission first.

✖ <u>**Video**</u> <u>**Hunt:**</u> The idea is to divide your group into groups of six or so, turn them loose across your city with a video camera and a list of stuff to film the group doing. The possibilities are limitless. Here are a few that youth ministers have sent to each other

across the Internet (Obviously, some of these will require prior permission; at least tell the groups to ask first!):

❶ Video of group member up against a police car being frisked and cuffed. Bonus points if it is an adult chaperone; no points at all if the group member actually does something to get arrested.

❷ Video the group at a unique city landmark.

❸ Video of the group building a pyramid in the canned food section of the supermarket. This one is fun because some groups will make a pyramid of canned foods; others will make a pyramid of themselves in the aisle.

Skitzophrenia

Divide youth into small groups of five or six. Give each team a large bag filled with various items. The group must then go make up a skit using all the props in the bag. The props can include anything. Suggested items: a light bulb, a stapler, a trash can, balls of various sizes, a jump rope, fruit, hats, ties, sporting equipment, a ream of unopened paper, or any item you could quickly throw in a bag. You can suggest a theme which the skit must be developed around or leave the skits open. The teams are given fifteen or twenty minutes to plan. Ask each team to present their skit to the large group.

Sneakers

This is an incredible night game. For this game you need a building with a flat roof and one or two entrance doors unlocked. Two or three participants go to the roof with flashlights or flood lights (if you have a power source). The large group has five minutes or less to hide away from the building at least 100 feet or more. They may hide in the bushes, in trees, in dumpsters, cars, and so forth On the signal, players hiding try to sneak into the open entrances of the building without being spotted by the players on the roof. The players on the roof search with their lights for the people sneaking into the building. When they see someone, they call out that person's name. If the group is very large and members do not know each other's names, use the rule that anyone who is touched by the light and knows he or she has been spotted must be honest and surrender. The first two or three to make it safely into the building without being seen get to be on the roof next.

Snow Blitz

This is a great fellowship for a hot summer afternoon. The motif is snow and ice. Decorate with snowflakes, snowmen, skis, ice skates or any other items which set the mood of winter. Possible games include: (1) a snowball fight using white plastic foam balls; (2) ice block races where youth sit on the ice blocks and slide down a hill; (3) ski races using old shoes or boots nailed to boards; (4) ice fishing where youth must dig through a bucket of crushed ice to find the "fish." Refreshments can include ice cream, snow cones, and other cold snacks.

Super Bowl Party

One church solved the problem of missing the first half of the Super Bowl because of evening worship services by using two VCR's. For the after-church fellowship, they watched the first half on tape while the second half was going on, then switched tapes.

Swing into Spring

This is a great fellowship after a long winter of being indoors. Begin with a kite event. Provide supplies and have youth make their own kites. You may give awards for the best flight, most unusual, longest tail, and so forth. Plan various types of races associated with the things of spring. You may have a tricycle race or lawn mowing race. There could be a tree climbing contest or flower planting or picking contest. Think of other items associated with spring and make up your own fun!

Table Game Night

This is a great fellowship idea for a winter night or during bad weather when other plans have to be canceled. Set up card tables and chairs and various games on each table. When youth arrive, instruct them to sit down where there is an empty chair around the game tables. On the signal, each table has ten or fifteen minutes to play their game. At the end of the time limit, the table needs to find a way to recognize the winner. The winner stays at that game while the rest of the players move to a new table and new game. The purpose is not to complete or win games as much as it is to move youth from their comfort zones. As youth move to new games they are forced to play and talk with new members or youth who are not in their usual crowd. At the end of the night, recognize anyone who stayed at the same table in the same game, i.e., someone who won every time. Recognize anyone who has played every game, i.e., lost every time and so moved to each table during the evening, too!

T.A.G.—"The Assassination Game"

This is a great game that can last all week at a youth camp or on a mission trip. Each youth participating gets the name of someone else who is playing, called a "contract." The game organizer makes sure that no two people have each

other's names at the beginning. Everyone has a toy gun that shoots rubber darts. The object is to "rub out" the person whose name you have.

Here are the rules:
- ✖ A kill can be made only when there are no witnesses.
- ✖ The game can be played only during free time—it is suspended during worship services, while the group is on mission projects, and so forth. (Modify this rule to fit the situation.)
- ✖ When you have been assassinated, you must give your "contract" (the person you were going after) to the person who killed you. Your killer then turns in his "contract" on you to the game organizer, who posts it on a central bulletin board.

The game will eventually come down to just two people, stalking each other. One particular group had great fun with the game. The game organizer gave each "assassin" a secret-agent type profile, complete with aliases, crimes they had committed, and so forth. When it got down to two people, both of them actually paid other people to be constant witnesses to their every move, because as long as someone was watching them, they couldn't be shot!

Tailgate Party

Before home football games at the high school, park your church bus or van in the stadium parking lot, bring a portable sound system to blast Christian music, and serve barbecue from the bus for whoever comes by. This could be an effective outreach event as well as a fun fellowship.

Treasure Hunt

Hide clues in different places around town. Each clue has a letter with it, and the letters spell out the location of a youth fellowship. You may want to hide some clues at stores in the mall, and ask the store manager to give the next clue only if the youth do some stunt first. Each team will need a responsible adult driver to drive them around; if they get stumped, they can dial a help line (a youth par-

ent or church secretary) who will give them the next clue. A youth minister who masterminded this event had small groups getting the clues in a different order, which made it less of a race to get to a certain clue. Or you can actually give the groups different sets of clues.

31 Flavor Taste-Off

Get one quart of each of the Baskin-Robbins flavors. Youth are given a numbered list. They sample each flavor (this involves lots of those little sample spoons), and they have to determine the name of each of the different ice cream flavors.

Tidy Bowl

This is an all-afternoon football tournament held on one Sunday after church. The only requirement for partic-ipants is to be in Bible study that morning. For one church, it was a great way to get unchurched youth into Bible study, and teachers made sure the lesson was highly evangelistic that morning.

Toilet Bowl Derby

Divide youth into teams. Each team must build a non-motorized Toilet-mobile. Old toilets can usually be found at a junk yard. This ends up being a strange looking go-cart type machine. Youth may decorate the Toilet-mobile any way they wish. The Toilet-mobiles are then entered in a race. One person must sit on the toilet and two people are allowed to push. Youth must devise a way to steer the toilet, as well as build it well enough so it does not fall apart during the race. The prize for the winner of the derby may be a decorated plunger!

True/False

This is a great game which works like a quiz game. Divide the large group into two teams. Ask the two teams to line up facing

one another. One team is the "TRUE" team, the other team is the "FALSE" team. The leader reads statements which are either true or false. If the statement is true, the TRUE team must turn around and run to their "base" at least twenty-five feet away. The FALSE team members try to tag the TRUE team members. If a person is tagged before reaching the safe point, that individual must become a team member on the opposite team. If the statement is false, the FALSE team members try to reach their base before being tagged by the TRUE team members. The true/false statements may be Bible related or might be based on a recent Bible study or sermon. You may play either for a specific time period or until most of the members are on one team. If you have enough questions and the teams continue to change because of tagging, this game could go on forever!

Sample true/false statements:
1 Moses took two of every animal on the ark. (Answer: false—Noah was captain of the ark, not Moses.)
2 Jesus said, "I am the Way, the Truth and the Life." (Answer: true—John 14:6)
3 Jesus used bread and chicken to feed the 5,000. (Answer: false—Matthew 14:17)

Be creative and have fun!

Turkey Bowl

There were actually two radically different ideas submitted with the name "Turkey Bowl." Both of them are good.

Version 1: A huge, well-organized youth flag football game over the Thanksgiving break, complete with a striped field, uniformed referees, and modified coed rules. After The Game (and you have to capitalize "The Game"), have a big turkey sandwich fellowship.

Version 2: The Wednesday night before Thanksgiving, roll long strips of heavy plastic down the floor of your fellowship hall. At one end, arrange ten pins. Youth stand at the other end and hurl frozen turkeys at the pins. Keep score. High scorers get the turkey. Moms who cooked the turkeys the next day claimed that the meat had been extra tenderized from the workout it got.

Turn on the TV

Here is a super event for Halloween, but it is fun at any other time of the year. Ask youth to come dressed up as their favorite TV char-

acter, past or present. You can have the large group vote on the costumes, and then announce the ratings. Activities might include singing favorite television theme songs. Play takeoffs of TV game shows ("Name That Tune," "Family Feud," "Jeopardy," and so forth). Skits that make fun of soap operas or sitcoms are always a hit. You may also want to show out-takes of differ- ent television shows available at local video stores. Of course, you will want to serve TV dinners. It would be great to videotape the entire event and play it back to the youth at another time.

Video Fellowship /Night of a Thousand Stars

Meet early in the day on a Saturday— give small groups of stu- dents a list of characters and some possible scenarios. Then have them go off and make movies that afternoon. That night all groups come back and watch the movies together. Offer Academy Award- style awards—Best Actor, Best Actress, Best Picture, and so forth (But be sure to give an award to everyone!).

Yuck Night

Youth bring a clean change of clothes, and play lots and lots of dirty games. You can do shaving cream fights, flour-sock fights, Hershey syrup fights, and so forth. You can set up a Jello slip-and- slide using long sheets of plastic, and a mud volleyball court. The possibilities are endless!

Group Building Ideas

Our job as youth workers is to build up the body of Christ through youth ministry. How do we go about this bodybuilding? It happens on two levels. First, there is group bodybuilding. How do you build attendance? How do you shake your group out of its apathy? How do you promote your student ministry? In this section, you will find some great ideas to help reach those goals.

Possibly the more important but often neglected dimension of bodybuilding is the building up of individuals within the body. How do you reach out to hurting youth? How do you let them know that you are available to them and responsive to their needs? How do you equip and train youth to be the church? In this chapter, look for some valuable ideas in these areas as well.

The important thing is balance. Do not get so caught up in building the big group that you lose sight of individuals. Also, don't spend so much time with individuals that others in the group begin to suspect you are playing favorites. Enough sermonizing. On with the ideas!

A Person of Great Worth

With one bag of Werther's candy, you can make a lasting impression on your group. Use Hebrews 3:13 and Hebrews 10:25 to set the mood for an encouragement time. Use a single, gold-wrapped piece of

Werther's candy to illustrate a person's "Werth" in God's eyes.

- ✖ Werther's are wrapped in gold—a precious metal. Each person is precious in God's sight.
- ✖ If you hold the wrapper up to the light, you can see through it. God still loves us, even though He can see right through us when we are held up to His light.
- ✖ Of course, the best part of the candy is not the shiny outside, but the sweet inside. Outside appearances can be deceiving. All that glitters is not gold, but all that is gold does not glitter.

You can then go to the youth one at a time and tell them that they are a person of great worth as you hand them a piece of the candy. Or you can have the youth go to each other and tell why they see each other as people of great worth.

Big Brothers/Big Sisters

Youth need community with one another, but they don't always know how to initiate it. Here is an idea that helped make new members in the youth group feel right at home. Assign each younger youth to an older youth. Give them times to pray together, eat together, and talk together. Let them share struggles with one another. You can do this short-term, through the duration of a choir tour or youth camp, or you can go longer term, such as for the first semester of the school year. Not only was this idea great for the younger members, but it also helped older ones know how much they were being looked up to.

Bus Benches

A church in Sacramento, California, has had great success promoting their student ministry on bus benches. They rent the bench for about $15 per month, with a three month minimum. The set-up fee for the decal that goes on the bench is $90. This church rented a bench directly across the street from the front door of the high school. Students could not help but see it every day of the school year.

Camp Mailbox

When you are at camp, have a mailbox in your main meeting room. Provide stacks of scrap paper and pencils. The idea is that during free times throughout the week— before and after group meetings while everyone is still gathering, youth can write notes of encouragement to each other. Different people volunteer to deliver mail before each group time.

C.H.A.M.P.

One church developed this as a five-point discipleship and account-ability program. Those who stayed faithful to all five points during the time of the study were given a "C.H.A.M.P." Award:

C onsistent in Bible Study
H elpful at Home
A ctive in Church
M otivated at School
P ersonal Witness

Claim Your Heritage

This group-building activity is designed to help youth recognize their family heritage, as well as letting others in the youth group know where they are "coming from." Each person is instructed to bring one item that represents his or her ancestry. This item might be a photo, an heirloom, or an interesting story about their family. Encourage youth to find out about their family trees. Ask the group to share what items and qualities they would like to pass down through the generations to their descendants. Allow for plenty of discussion and sharing.

Coat of Arms

Instruct youth to design a coat of arms. Explain that the coat of arms should symbolize the purpose of their youth group. The group

can include three or four words which describe their goals and things which are most important to them as a whole. Ask youth to think about their greatest achievement as a large group. Ask them to think about how they hope others see them as a youth group. The final emblem can be used on mail outs, publicity at church, or maybe even T-shirts.

College Corner

Set up a designated corner in the church, church library, or the senior high Bible study area. Provide a table, chairs, and possibly a bookshelf. Contact colleges, universities, seminaries, and vocational training institutes and ask them to send their current school catalog. Request that they also send admissions and financial aid information. Display all the catalogs and other information in the college corner. Not only will youth become informed about their options after high school, but parents, current college students, and potential students will use the corner.

To enhance the college corner, plan several day trips to visit various colleges and universities in your area or state. Set up the days and times you will visit the campuses. Plan a campus tour where youth and/or their parents can see the dorms, library, student center, and specific buildings. This is a great way to minister to the youth and their parents when they are making this major decision about life and vocation. Pray with the group at the end of the visit. Pray that their decisions will be based on God's will and plan for them.

Community Parades

Several groups have entered floats in their town's Fourth of July parade. It is a great way to promote the group, and the youth have a good time working together on the float.

Coupon Books

Design and print small coupon books for your group. Give one book to each person in the group. These coupon book can be used anytime, but work especially well on a retreat or mission trip. The coupons read "Good for one hug," "Good for one hike," "Good

for one meal sitting together," "Good for one sleeping bag rolled up," and so forth. The only rules are (1) the coupon has to be redeemed when asked, and (2) a different person must redeem each of your coupons. These are great for getting youth to interact with one another.

Dial-a-Prayer

Organize a prayer chain among the members of the youth group. Assign one person as the lead caller. This person is the one to call with any prayer requests. Make sure all the youth have this person's phone number. The lead caller then calls the number of the person next in the chain and shares the prayer request. Each person in the prayer chain is then given another member's name and phone number to call. The last person in the chain calls the lead caller to assure that the prayer chain is complete. Encourage youth in the prayer chain to call the person with the initial prayer request. Explain that it is important to let that person know you are really praying for him or her. Encourage youth to also share words of encouragement and Scripture with the person requesting prayer.

Do You Know Yourself?

As youth arrive, give each person the name of someone else in the group. Explain that during the next thirty minutes, they are to speak and act like that person. They are to assume the name of that person. They are to make statements from their knowledge of the person and answer questions as they think that person would answer. Follow up with a discussion of the experience. This can help youth understand what they are like from the point of view of their peers.

Encouragement Team

Ask for volunteers or assign specific youth each quarter to serve as the encouragement team. This group of youth will write notes of encouragement, send birthday cards, give special recognition, and other uplifting things weekly. The encouragement team can contact anyone in the group who missed a church activity. It is a great way to provide for accountability within the group. More importantly, an encouragement team helps to make sure no one is left out or lost among the masses.

Fragile Friendships

This group-building activity helps youth to realize the fragileness of friendships and the importance of caring for one another. This can be used anytime, but it works great on a retreat.

Give each person a raw egg. Instruct youth to punch a small hole in each end of the egg with a pin. Then direct them to blow on one end of the egg. All the contents will be forced out the other end, leaving an empty, unbroken eggshell. You may seal up the holes with a small amount of candle wax.

Discuss the delicate nature of eggshells. Relate this to the fragile nature of friendships. Discuss various ways we hurt or break our friends (in the areas of trust, love, faithfulness, honesty, and so forth). Then give each person in the group a thin-point marker that will write on the eggshells. Ask youth to write the names of several of their friends or family members on the eggshell. They need to be very careful not to break the egg while doing this writing.

Explain that each person must carry around and care for his or her egg for the rest of the day. Allow youth to provide some form of protection while accepting responsibility for the egg's condition. At the end of the day, ask everyone to present the eggs. Discuss the feelings of responsibility and the problems with protecting something so fragile. Discuss ways the group can avoid hurting one another in the future.

Friendship Notes

Prepare some index cards (or slips of paper). Print the beginning of the sentences to start the thought and leave the ending blank. Be sure to leave room for youth to write in their thoughts. Possible printed messages might be: "I was thinking about you and..."; "You are special to me because..."; "I always look forward to seeing you because..."; or other messages appropriate for your group. These cards can be available at a designated time or at any time.

  This could be a special activity to begin a Bible study or fellowship time. Write the name of each youth at the top of a card. Pass out the cards. Ask youth to fill in the blanks and give to the person whose name is on the top of the card. Ask youth to write encouraging and positive messages! This activity can really strengthen friendships in the group. Youth will sometimes write down thoughts they would never say to the person out loud!

Good Job, Babe!

Each week during one of the youth meetings, recognize one member of the group. Ask this person to come to the front of the room and sit on a stool. Tell the large group what a good job this person has been doing. You may want to recognize him or her for an accomplishment at church or school. Affirm this person openly and ask for three volunteers to share with the group why this person is special. Close by praying specifically for the individual. Thank God for her faithfulness and for being who He created her to be.

8
7

Group Scrapbook

At the beginning of the school year, explain that this year the group will be compiling a scrapbook. Ask youth to bring various items, photos, announcements, ticket stubs, worship bulletins, programs, or anything which represents activities of the youth group. At specific times during the year, have the group work together to compile the scrapbook pages. You may use regular photo albums or large poster board which can be fastened together into a book. During the last meeting of the year, display the youth scrapbook. Youth may even want to present the memories to the church body.

In addition to the scrapbook, you may want to develop a video scrapbook. Edit all the video footage from youth events throughout the year. Set the video to music. Present the video to the large group at the last youth meeting of the year. Give a copy of the video scrapbook to your graduating seniors as a gift. They will love it.

Honey Bee Award

Another fun thing to do at camp. Tape a paper honey bee on the bottom of one plate before students come in for dinner. Whoever gets the plate gets the award. They have to stand up and do something silly during the meal.

Leadership Retreat for Youth

A month or so before your youth Sunday, prepare the youth for taking leadership roles with this retreat. During the weekend, spend time on leadership studies and practical preparation for the coming event.

Memory Verse Mania

This is an incredible way to motivate youth to memorize Scripture. Memory Verse Mania works especially well on a retreat or some other event away from church. At the beginning of the retreat, divide youth into small groups and give each team a Bible verse.

There needs to be a good number of verses to memorize, so you may want to assign more than one to each team if you have a smaller group. The goal for each person is to learn as many verses as possible for individual points. Each team will receive a point for every person who learns the team's verse. During the retreat the verses may be part of a conversation, be hung on walls or doors, printed on toilet paper, put on pillows on beds, and so forth. Each team tries to teach its verse to the other youth who are part of the retreat. At the end of the retreat, everyone is to write down the verses they have learned. The person who has learned the most verses wins a prize, as does the team that has taught their verse to the most people. Youth can really use their imagination on this activity, and later they still know the verses.

Myself in a Box

Begin by giving each student a shoe box or another small box about the same size. Provide a large supply of magazines, newspapers, glue, scissors, markers, and so forth. Explain that they are to make a collage on the inside of the box that represents how they see themselves. Their feelings should be expressed through pictures, words, symbols, or whatever they believe represent themselves. On the outside of the box, youth should make a collage that represents how they believe others see them. If they want, they can let each side of the box represent how different people or groups of people see them (family, people at school, people at church, and so forth). After everyone has completed a box, divide into small groups and share the boxes (themselves) with each other. Close with a discussion of why there is a difference between the inside and the outside of the box (ourselves). Discuss why we hide our real feelings from others.

**101 IDEAS FOR OUTREACH AND EVANGELISM
IN YOUTH MINISTRY**

1. Sponsor a Nintendo tournament for younger youth.
2. Poll adults for the names of teens they know who are not currently involved in your church's youth ministry.
3. Ask youth to survey the block they live on for prospects.
4. Compare a list of recreation participants with Sunday School rolls.
5. Watch school announcements for newcomers.
6. When a youth is hospitalized, flood him or her with visits.
7. Visit the high school campus at lunch time (with permission).
8. Hold an annual "Youth Appreciation Day."
9. Do a telephone blitz to update Sunday School information on absentees and prospects.
10. Ask young adults if they know any baby-sitters that are not involved in a youth ministry.
11. Mingle at the mall with your youth, meet their friends.
12. Get involved in your school's drug and alcohol prevention programs for adolescents.
13. Use their Student DayMakers (a time-management system for students available by calling 800-458-2772) to help youth identify prospects.
14. Ye olde video party.
15. Poll parents to see if co-workers have teen-age children.
16. Enlist drivers for youth trips so you can spend road time visiting with teens.
17. Learn to "banter" with teens; this light-hearted fun can lead to more serious discussions later.
18. Create a working relationship with school guidance counselors (most beneficial in times of crisis).
19. Spend time discipling teens.
20. Invest time in training other youth workers, in order to multiply your outreach and evangelism efforts.
21. Substitute teach at your local school once a month.
22. Discover where teens are employed and drop by while they are working ...IF it's appropriate.
23. Ask youth about exchange students who may be interested in attending your group's activities.
24. "Gift Bag" for guests — fix up a bag with a soda, candy bar, an *essential connection* magazine or a student book, deliver to

home. (Magazine may be ordered by calling 800-458-2772.)

25. Be sure to have some sort of registration at every social or recreational event listing teen's name and phone number.

26. Network with other youth workers in your area. This enables you to work together to reach more teens.

27. "Pop Visitation"—Make a doorknob hanger with pertinent youth information. Hang it around a soda, drop it off at their home.

28. Create a "Youth Outreach Visitation Packet"—include a flyer about youth activities, student book, *Living with Teenagers* (a monthly for parents of teenagers which may be ordered by calling 800-458-2772), and so forth.

29. Satellite Sunday Schools—a couple of adults in outlying areas can start an Outreach Bible Study in their home.

30. TV Telethon—8 p.m. until 8 a.m.—Youth must bring a guest to attend. Include lots of board games and snacks.

31. In the summer hold your meetings outdoors—Tailgate Bible Study in the parking lot.

32. Volleyball extravaganza—beach balls, water balloons, and so forth.

33. Human Scavenger Hunt—List includes: blonde, straight A student, someone who just got a traffic ticket, and so forth.

34. Ye Olde Kidnap Breakfast: warn the parents and go get them!

35. Rent a racquetball court and have your group play Wallyball.

36. Offer to make wake-up calls during finals or for special days.

37. Appoint leaders in your youth group to make specific contacts.

38. Yard Commandoes fall service project—assemble pick-up trucks, tarps, rakes and plenty of teens; identify widows and others who need help.

39. When possible, on a home visit to meet a "new youth," take a youth member from the same school or neighborhood.

40. Power Bands—colored beads used as a witnessing tool.

41. Heaven Wall (at retreat or lock-in)—photocopy pictures of all the students in a school from yearbook(s), put all of them up on one wall. Challenge youth to move a picture to the opposite (Heaven) wall if they know for sure that person is a Christian. They must have talked with the student about his or her relationship to Christ; it's not enough to assume they are because they attend church. Then from the pictures remaining on the first wall, each youth picks one person to ask about their rela-

tionship to Christ.

42. Summer Pool School—start a Bible study at the pool.

43. Holy Rollers—Rollerblade or skateboard through neighborhoods, handing out flyers to an upcoming event.

44. The video camera gives you numerous opportunities to make your kids instant celebrities, to produce commercials for your meetings, and so on.

45. Big screen TV events—Super Bowl, World Series, and so on.

46. Lights Out time at camps and retreats can be a great time to share about God's love.

47. If morning is not your time, maybe a "Pizza Kidnap" would help you round up some new teens.

48. Watch newspapers for youth accomplishments, sports, choir, honor rolls, then drop the teen a note with a clipping.

49. Instant camera or audio cassette scavenger hunts can draw a crowd.

50. Don't underestimate the significance of remembering birthdays.

51. Show up at their ball games, recitals, and such. Get parents to help inform you of these events.

52. Back-to-School Burger Bash or The-Last-Blast-Before-Summer's-Past.

53. Youth Witness Training—train your teens to effectively share their faith through their own testimonies.

54. Lifesaver Night—do games with Lifesavers candy then talk about what we were "saved" from, "saved" for, and so forth.

55. Share copies of *essential connection* (see #24) when you meet teen prospects.

56. Big Time Balloon Blow-up—using helium balloons create balloon bouquets for recent guests, deliver the balloons, and invite them back.

57. Participate in your church's weekly visitation program, and take two or three teens out for a soft drink or frozen yogurt.

58. Plan an annual trip to a theme park or water park; use these as outreach times by offering cut rates to those who bring guests.

59. Would you believe ...a tie-dye party—have kids bring their own shirts, and tie-dye them. They'll have a blast.

60. Drop kids notes of encouragement.

61. Host a "Ping-Pong Night" — play a dozen different games

using variations of table tennis.

62. In the summer months, a "Messy Games" event can be a great way to get kids together—include eggs, flour, oatmeal, mud, and so forth.

63. A baby-sitting ministry can help teens reach out to adults and raise funds for other outreach events.

64. Invite prospects to a night of miniature golf and batting cages.

65. If your youth choir, drama, or puppet team performs in public settings, be sure you have flyers about your group to distribute.

66. Hold a "Read the Bible Through" marathon—from the pulpit; adults and youth sign up for half-hour slots. This takes three or four days.

67. "Blizzard Blitz"—play summer games in snow; for refreshments have Dairy Queen "Blizzards" or something similar.

68. Recruit and train "Care Group Leaders" in your Sunday School classes.

69. Take youth to camps like *Centrifuge* and *Crosspoint* where they are challenged to live evangelistic lifestyles.

70. Hold a "Soda Soak" with games like a belching contest, games using baby bottles, and so forth

71. Provide parenting tips for parents of your teens. If your church is holding *Parenting by Grace* classes, help advertise them.

72. Communicate clearly with the pastor and others who visit in homes so that they will let youth Sunday School teachers know if there are youth prospects.

73. Hold a hayride and bonfire in honor of new group members.

74. Contact your Associational ASSISTeam's youth specialist for help with reaching youth in your area.

75. "Snow-Daze" (like Yard Commandoes—just add snow!) Shovel the driveways and walks of the elderly and homes of prospective youth.

76. Reach out to the adventurous youth by sponsoring a camp-out, day hike, backpack, or float-trip; include daily Bible study.

77. Rent a public school gymnasium occasionally for group activities. It's not very expensive and involves just a little paperwork.

78. Have youth create "license plate" greetings and invitations to send to absentees and youth prospects—"MISN-U," for example.

79. Cooperate with para-church groups. They often look for

churches with youth ministry programs to plug kids into.

80. Be sensitive to special needs groups in your area: sight or hearing impaired, mentally challenged, and other similarly challenged teens.

81. Visit with former youth Sunday School teachers or youth minister to locate potential prospects who might have "dropped out."

82. Don't assume your kids know how to make a guest feel welcome. Do some role plays. Then discuss and prepare your teens for guests.

83. Utilize "cliques" in your group, and do events that target those groups, for example, cowboys, jocks, musicians.

84. Christmas caroling—find that area of town where everyone is driving to look at the lights and ask homeowners' permission to carol.

85. "Hammering Out the Truth"—promote a talk or meeting of the same name by mailing nails pushed through cards with information (check with the post office for requirements/surcharge).

86. "A penny for your thoughts"— Mail out letters with a penny attached, asking youth to bring ideas on how to promote an outreach event.

87. Get involved in team sports and leagues; get to know the participants; invite them to your activities.

88. Working with computers—your teens are often as knowledgeable about megabytes as you are. Get together and see what they can do.

89. Go with your kids to a local secular record store; you will discover "where they are at" and you'll probably meet a friend or two.

90. Get teens involved in a craft; encourage them to invite friends who might also enjoy that craft.

91. Have we mentioned a thoughtful letter? It's almost a lost art!

92. PRAY—This means everyone. Involve your group in praying for specific teens who need to know Christ.

93. GO FISH—Take them fishing, but don't forget to drop a hint or two about being fishers of men!

94. Become an authority on one or two hot youth topics and make yourself available to speak where your kids are. Examples are drugs, suicide, AIDS.

95. Have a few jokes or one liners ready when meeting teens'

friends. Leave them wondering, "Who was that guy?"

96. Send out goofy, bogus maps to members who haven't been to church in a while to help them "find their way back."

97. Send kids an audio- or videocassette message inviting them to your next meeting or event.

98. High school students can offer to tutor sixth and seventh graders.

99. A youth breakfast/get together before school. Encourage youth who ride with other kids to bring the whole carload.

100. Publish a one page "Roster" with all your teens' names and numbers, providing plenty of space for names of new members.

101. Finally, showing interest in whatever they are "into" and being available to spend time with them will show that you care.

This list was compiled by Jeff Buscher, Kalispell, MT, and updated by Bob Metcalf, Nashville, TN. Used here by permission.

For more ways to reach youth, see *Ideas For Reaching Youth* by Knierim, Vickie, Craig Fry, and Bob Metcalf (Convention Press, 1992, 5271-14); *Idea Books* from Youth Specialties and *Group Growers* from Group Publishing.

Ongoing SYATP

In one church, the youth took it upon themselves to continue "See You at the Pole" throughout the year. SYATP was on September 10 the first year the group participated. So they met at the flagpole on the tenth of every month.

Operation A.F.C.

A church in Arlington, Texas, used the following concept to build the youth group during the often-drab winter months. They used a manual to lay out the entire rationale and plan of action for the project. By adopting a military motif, the group got extremely excited about evangelism, outreach, and group building. Dates on the following pages illustrate the time periods used—the plan could work at another time, too.

Arlington for Christ
February 5—February 26, 1995

PURPOSE
Operation A.F.C. is a tool used to accomplish the following:
1. Reach teenagers for Christ.
2. Teach them that Bible study can be fun and life-changing.
3. Give them an incentive to memorize Scripture.
4. Create unity within the youth group.
5. Create excitement during a particularly slow month for our church.

SQUADS
A. Squads will begin with the same number of people. These people will be selected by the Captains two weeks prior to the beginning of the operation.

B. New squad members may be added on a first come, first served basis.

C. Squad members may change squads if the change is made by Sunday, February 5, the beginning of OPERATION A.F.C. This change must be in writing and submitted to the Commanding Officer. 10,000 points will be deducted from your squad for each change.

D. Plan and operate an OPERATION A.F.C. Event. (See Sergeant's Job Description).

E. Find a name for your squad and create a military type chant.

CAPTAINS:
A. Captains are to call Sergeant, Corporal, and every Private each of the four weeks of OPERATION A.F.C. During the call:
1. Encourage them to have a daily quiet time with God.
2. Encourage them to attend all youth group activities.
3. Encourage each squad member to invite at least one person to each youth group activity.
4. Pray over the phone with them for their needs and the needs of the other squad members.

B. See that the Sergeant is planning an OPERATION A.F.C. Event following these rules:
   1. The Event can be any time your squad wants it to be between February 5 and February 26.
   2. The event can be anything fun you want to do (anything Christ would approve).
   3. To qualify for an OPERATION A.F.C. Event:
      a. All squad members should be present. You will be docked points for each member NOT present.
      b. The youth minister or a Sunday School worker must be contacted BEFORE the event. Leave a message on answering machines if you are unable to talk directly to them.
      c. Spend some time in prayer—share prayer requests and pray for them. Note: Everyone does not have to pray out loud, but that would be desirable.
      d. If a Sunday School teacher or the youth minister is invited, extra points will be given.

C. See that the Corporal records the attendance of each squad member for each youth group event or meeting. The attendance sheets must be placed in the proper folder outside the youth minister's office to assure credit for their attendance. If your Corporal is not present, it is your responsibility to appoint someone to this task or do it yourself.

D. Each week assign members a prayer partner.

E. Commit, for sure, to come to Sunday School each Sunday for the four Sundays of OPERATION A.F.C.

F. Plus the responsibilities of the Privates.

SERGEANTS:
A. Plan and operate an OPERATION A.F.C. Event:
   1. The Event can be any time your squad wants it to be between February 5 and February 26.
   2. The event can be anything fun you want to do (anything Christ would approve).

3. To qualify for an OPERATION A.F.C. Event:
   a. All members should be there. You will be docked points for each member NOT present.
   b. The youth minister or a Sunday School worker must be contacted BEFORE the event. Leave a message on answering machines if you are unable to talk directly to them.
   c. Spend some time in prayer—share prayer requests and pray for them. Note: Everyone does not have to pray out loud, but that would be desirable.
4. If a Sunday School teacher or the youth minister is invited, extra points will be given.

B. Commit, for sure, to come to Sunday School each Sunday for the four Sundays of OPERATION A.F.C.

C. Plus the responsibilities of the Privates.

CORPORALS:

A. The Corporals will be responsible for recording the attendance of each squad member.
B. The attendance sheets must be placed in the proper folder outside the youth minister's office to assure credit for their attendance.
C. Commit, for sure, to come to Sunday School each Sunday for the four Sundays of OPERATION A.F.C. and Youth Prayer Groups.
D. Plus the responsibilities of the Privates.

PRIVATES:

A. Privates commit to attend church activities at least two times a week for the next four weeks. This would include: Sunday School, choir, Sunday evening worship, Discipleship, youth prayer groups, visitation, and/or weekend activities.
B. Commit to try to do a quiet time with God daily.
C. Pray for your prayer partner daily.
D. Commit to live the Christlike life at school and after school.
E. When a squad member is being attacked by the enemy

(Satan), go talk to them about God's love and forgiveness.

F. Commit to invite at least one non-member to come with you to youth group activities.

CIVILIAN/AWOL

A. A civilian is a visitor. A visitor is anyone who is not a member of Arlington's Sunday School.

B. A squad will get points for three weeks of consecutive attendance for each civilian.

C. After three weeks, the squad members should encourage the civilian to join Sunday School. They may (and should) join even before the third week.

> **Note:** One does not have to be "saved" in order to become a Sunday School member. However, in order to be a church member, he or she does have to be "saved" and baptized.

D. If they do not wish to become Sunday School members, they will earn the same number of points as do squad members.

E. An AWOL is a Sunday School member who has not been in Sunday School 15% of the time since July 3, 1994.

F. AWOL's will earn visitor points for the Squad who brings them, but not new member points when they become active.

NEW MEMBER:

A. New Members are those who decide to join Sunday School.

B. New Members are then counted as members.

C. New Members to your squad will be encouraged to go to the incentive trip during spring break with the youth group.

SCRIPTURE MEMORY:

A. Points will be given for each verse of Scripture memorized.

B. To receive points, the squad member must tell the verse to a youth worker or to the youth minister. Cut the card out and give it to the youth worker to listen to your verse. After you have said the verse word for word, he or she will sign your card.

C. You may memorize and recite the verse out of any Biblical

translation you choose. Write the verse on the back of the card in that translation.

D. If you are memorizing verses for another church program, you may substitute those for the ones on your card. However, the verse must be written on the back of a card to receive points.

Note: hand grenades will be thrown from the list of Scriptures below.

E. Memorize the following verses. (These verses are printed here for your convenience out of the King James Version. Feel free to memorize out of any translation—see C. above.):

1. Isaiah 59:2   *But your iniquities have separated between you and your God, and your sins have hid his face from you, that he will not hear.*

2. Romans 3:23   *For all have sinned, and come short of the glory of God;*

3. Romans 6:23   *For the wages of sin is death; but the gift of God is eternal life through Jesus Christ our Lord.*

4. John 3:16   *For God so loved the world, that he gave his only begotten Son, that whosoever believeth in him should not perish, but have everlasting life.*

5. John 10:10   *The thief cometh not, but for to steal, and to kill, and to destroy: I am come that they might have life, and that they might have it more abundantly.*

6. Romans 5:8   *But God commendeth his love toward us, in that, while we were yet sinners, Christ died for us.*

7. 1 Peter 3:18   *For Christ also hath once suffered for sins, the just for the unjust, that he might bring us to God, being put to death in the flesh, but quickened by the Spirit:*

8. John 14:6   *Jesus saith unto him, I am the way, the truth, and the life: no man cometh unto the Father, but by me.*

9. Ephesians 2:8-9   *For by grace are ye saved*

through faith; and that not of yourselves: it is the gift of God: Not of works, lest any man should boast.

10. John 1:12   *But as many as received him, to them gave he power to become the sons of God, even to them that believe on his name:*

11. Revelation 3:20   *Behold, I stand at the door, and knock: if any man hear my voice, and open the door, I will come in to him, and will sup with him, and he with me.*

Hand Grenades:

In an effort to keep Scripture before each soldier in the Lord's army, Sunday School teachers or the youth minister can throw a hand grenade at any soldier at any time. Youth workers, in order to be fair, throw your hand grenades equally to all squads.

A. A hand grenade is when the Sunday School teacher hands one of the above verses on the hand grenade card to a soldier.

B. If the soldier knows the verse, triple points will be given. This is called a Totally Disabled Hand Grenade.

C. If the soldier does not know the particular verse handed to him but can quote another verse either on the list or on a list he is memorizing for another church program, he will be awarded 5,000 points. Write the reference of the verse on the back of the card. This is called a Partially Disabled Hand Grenade.

D. If the soldier does not know the particular verse and cannot recall any of the verses on the list, his squad will be docked 1,000 points. This is called a Direct Hit.

Note to the youth workers: You may help the members with a few words to jog their memory on the hand grenade verses. Remember, the point is to hide God's word in our hearts, not to embarrass people because they don't happen to know the particular verse you give to them.

101

<u>POINTS</u>

Event	Day & Time	Member	CIVILIAN/M.I.A.
Sunday School	Sun 9:15 & 10:45	5,000	10,000
Youth Choir	Sun 5:15 P.M.	7,000	10,000
Visitation	Mon 7:00 P.M.	7,000	10,000
Karate	Mon 5:00 P.M.	5,000	10,000

Basketball Sunday

Event	Day & Time	Member	CIVILIAN/M.I.A.
School Outreach	Mon 7:00 P.M.	5,000	10,000
S.W.A.T. Night	Wed 6:15	7,000	20,000
Youth Prayer Groups	Fri 7:27 P.M. Sharp	10,000	20,000

DiscipleNow

Event	Day & Time	Member	CIVILIAN/M.I.A.
Thursday	Feb. 16, - 7:00 P.M.	15,000	25,000
Friday	Feb. 17 - 7:00 P.M.	15,000	25,000
Banquet/Concert	Feb. 18 - 5:30 P.M.	15,000	25,000
Sunday School	Feb. 19 - both times	10,000	20,000
Assoc. Choir Rehea	Feb. 20 - 9:00 A.M.	10,000	20,000
City Wide Yth Crusa	Feb. 23 - 6:30 P.M.	15,000	30,000
City Wide Yth Crusa	Feb. 24 - 6:301	5,000	30,000
City Wide Yth Crusa	Feb. 25 - 6:30	15,000	30,000

New member.	30,000
Bible brought.	1,000
Scripture memorized.	10,000
Hand-grenade - - Total Disabled	30,000
Hand grenade - - Partially Disabled	5,000
Hand-grenade - - blown to kingdom come	1,000
Call and leave your name and . . . . squad name on Youth Hotline	1,000
Each member called by Captain. . . . . (Captains call each of their members.)	5,000
Paid deposit to summer camp due no later than Feb.	2630,000
Paid deposit to mission trip due no later than Feb.	2630,000
Paid deposit for the retreat due no later than Feb.	2630,000

OPERATION A.F.C. EVENT

Any time you want and as many times as you want (see Sergeant's responsibilities).

Members	5,000
AWOL	10,000
CIVILIAN	10,000
Squad	30,000

Remember Operation A.F.C. is only a tool for the Arlington Baptist Church Youth to accomplish the Great Commission: *And Jesus came and spake unto them, saying, "All power is given unto me in heaven and in earth. Go ye therefore, and teach all nations, baptizing them in the name of the Father, and of the Son, and of the Holy Ghost: Teaching them to observe all things whatsoever I have commanded you: and, lo, I am with you alway, even unto the end of the world. Amen."* Matthew 28:18-20

Editor's note: Some characteristics of this game were changed to make the procedures clearer for general audiences.

Peek-a-boo Box

This simple idea is a wonderful way to get youth to read bulletin board information. Build a box out of plywood about three feet wide by three feet deep by three feet high. Mount it on legs and cut a hole in the bottom. The hole should be big enough for one of your youth to stick his or her head through. Paint and decorate the outside of the box or ask youth to decorate it. One side of the box should be hinged, so that it will open up but can then be shut and locked. Place a small battery-operated light inside. On the inside of the box, hang flyers, brochures, announcements, posters, photos and other items of information or interest. Youth must get under the box and place their heads through the opening in the bottom in order to see what is inside. Although youth might normally ignore announcements on a bulletin board, they will line up to see what is inside the box. It is best if you change the box every week or two to keep up the momentum. You can use the box at your church only or try taking it to place where youth spend extra time. Just make sure you have permission to display the box, even if it is a "public" place.

A fun variation of the peek-a-boo box is to place a black light inside instead of the regular light. Make all of your signs and announcements with fluorescent markers or paints. This is a great change and keeps your youth curious about what will be in the box next week.

Photo Postcards

This idea is a wonderful way to communicate various messages to members of your youth group. Using a 35mm camera, take several photos of each member of the group. Take photos of the youth in small groups, in prayer, in Bible studies, during activities at church, at extra-curricular activities at school, and so forth. Be sure to take a photo of any visitor with several of the other youth. When you have the film developed, ask for 4-by-6-inch size prints. Then use the photos as postcards to communicate with the group. You can remind visitors of their experience with the youth group with few words and a great picture. You can send congratulations, words of encouragement, announcements of upcoming events, or any other message to the youth in your group. The youth will love the photo and all the memories it evokes.

P.O.P. Stars

An intercessory prayer ministry for your youth group. P.O.P. stands for Power of Prayer. The idea is to have every single one of your students and group leaders prayed for every single day of the year.

With a spreadsheet program, create a cell for each week of the year. Then, begin to fill in your students' and workers' names from the Sunday School roll. Depending on the size

THE
ANSWER
TO YOUR
PRAYERS

of your group, you may have several students in each cell, or you may have a student prayed for more than once in the year. Print this first copy, and mark it with a "1" in the upper right corner. Now, using the cut and paste feature on your software, move the names in each cell forward one week: the January Week One name moves to January Week Two, Week Two to Week Three, and so on. Move the names in Week Four of December to Week One of January. Print this one, mark it "2" and repeat the process. Continue until you have fifty-two packets.

Now, recruit fifty-two adults in your church to serve as POP Stars. Each one gets a packet, and thus through-out the year, all of your students are prayed for on a daily basis. Send a newsletter out to your POP Stars each month, informing them of new members in the youth group and where to add them on the charts. You may also recruit two of your POP Stars to pray through your youth Bible study each week.

POP CALENDAR 1998 #1		
Week 1	**Jan 4-10**	**John Doe**
Week 2	**Jan 11-17**	**Mary Low**
Week 3	**Jan 18-24**	**Bob So**
	on through . . .	
Week 51	**Dec 20-26**	**Jane Joe**
Week 52	**Dec 27-Jan 2**	**Ann Mo**

Then shift the entire column of names down one space and print copy 2.

POP CALENDAR 1998 #2		
Week 1	Jan 4-10	Ann Mo
Week 2	Jan 11-17	John Doe
Week 3	Jan 18-24	Mary Low
Week 4	Jan 25-24	Bob So
	on through . . .	
Week 51	Dec 20-26	Bill Bow
Week 52	Dec 27-Jan 2	Jane Joe

Remember to move the last name back to the first week in January before you run the next list.

Then shift again and get copy 3, and so on. This way, there will be 52 POP Stars and everyone will be prayed for every week.

Prayer Candles

Ask the large group to sit in a circle in a darkened room or outside at night. Give each person one unlit candle. One person has a lit candle. The person with the lit candle prays silently or aloud for another member in the circle. After completing the prayer, that person goes over to the person he or she just prayed for and lights that person's candle. He or she returns to a place in the circle with the lighted candle. The one whose candle was just lit then prays for another person in the circle and then goes to light that person's candle. This continues until all the candles are lit. At the end of the prayer time, the group leader closes in prayer. All the candles can then be blown out simultaneously.

Prayer Pagers

Each member of the group is assigned a personal code number. For example, Joe Smith might be "#16." They are given a card with their code number and the youth minister's pager number on the front, plus basic directions. On the back is a list of 28 possible prayer concerns (generic) such as *1 — test today, 2 — game today, 3 — parent problems*, and so forth. They call the youth minister's pager number, enter their code number, then the star button for a dash and then the number of their request; and then the pound button to send. The youth minister gets the message: "16-1." This lets the youth minister know that Joe has a test today. The minister stops and prays for him throughout the day and then contacts him within a couple days to see how it went. The group may develop codes for kids who just want to say "Hi" and for those who want to let the youth minister know what time their games are.

Prayer Walk

This works especially well with smaller groups (twenty or less) on a retreat. Prior to the walk set up a trail with specific places marked as stopping points. It would be great if each stopping point had something which represented a specific person in the group. The group walks silently from place to place. At each stopping point, one person from the group shares specific prayer requests. The group prays for that person at that spot. By the end of the prayer walk, each member of the group has shared his or her prayer requests and had the group pray for them. Everyone seems to know each other a little better after a prayer walk.

Round Robin Letters

These letters are fun and helpful at the same time. Begin by dividing youth into small groups of no more than five. Explain that one person in the group is to start the letter, writing to other members in the group. That person then mails the letter to the next person in the group. This person writes or adds on to the same letter. He or she then encloses all that has been written and mails the letter to the third person. This continues until everyone has read and written the letter. When the letter comes full circle, the starting writer throws away the old part of his or her letter and begins again. This is very

effective if one of the members in the group is a missionary or foreign exchange student. It is fun for them to receive a letter that is four or five pages long with lots of information.

Study Hall

At different times during the school year, youth may feel especially stressed and pressured. On the Sundays or other days of the week prior to these stress weeks (midterms, final exams, and so forth), youth may be struggling trying to decide whether or not they should attend church and youth activities. Many youth feel they should stay home and study. One way to minister to your group during these times is to set up a study hall at the church. Youth can come for their regular church activities (choir, discipleship, worship services) and then, instead of a program or fellowship, extend the time and designate it for study. Provide some refreshments and plenty of tables and chairs. Design the room so that students with the same classes can review and study together, but also provide space for those who need to study alone. Possibly enlist some teachers or knowledgeable adults to be available to tutor during this time. A lot can be accomplished during these study hall hours. Make sure to monitor the room; those who are not studying need to leave!

Thank-You Notes

Youth are often better at writing down their thoughts than expressing them aloud. Writing thank-you notes can be a great group-building activity any time of the year. It also can be done in conjunction with a Bible study during the Thanksgiving holidays. Buy some nice thank-you notes from a local stationery store or department store. Distribute the notes among the youth. Ask youth to write thank-you notes to each other, their parents, youth leaders, specific members at church, and so forth. (Decide before the session on a group to receive the thank-you notes.) Mail or hand deliver the notes at an appropriate time.

Thursday Lunch Club

If you are in a community that allows students to go off campus for lunch, you might consider a program like this. One California church directly across from a high school fed almost 300 students a week last year with this program. They do not charge the students but make it a time for relationship building. There is a volunteer staff of six people that help the youth minister every week. The menus consist of several different items and are rotated throughout the semester. This one event each week has proven to be the biggest magnet to the youth ministry of this church. It costs on the average around $60.00 each week to feed 300 kids. Each week youth fill out cards for the door prizes. On these cards are boxes in which they can check different outreach questions, such as, "I am interested in becoming a member of the church," "I have a prayer request," or "I would like to talk to a pastor." These cards are followed up on each week. At the last week of school, twelve youth indicated they were interested in becoming a Christian. Door prizes are candy bars, soft drinks, and, if there is a trip coming up, a free trip at each lunch. The Thursday lunch youth are integrated well into the rest of the church ministry. They are on the mailing list for the youth newsletter, and youth events are also advertised in the school paper.

Unfinished Sentences

Unfinished sentences are used to stimulate discussion before a Bible study or at any time. Youth can express and explore their beliefs and values as they are challenged to complete the sentences. This can be done in small discussion groups or by giving each youth a piece of paper and pencil. Emphasize that there are no restrictions on the content of the sentences; there are not necessarily any right or wrong answers. The emphasis is on the spontaneous true reflections of each individual, and they should be as honest as possible. Each person also has the right to pass rather than give the answer aloud. This activity works best if members of the group know each

other well. The more serious the group remains, the more likely they will develop a stronger atmosphere of freedom and trust among themselves. You can use any unfinished sentence to begin your discussion. Here are some unfinished sentences which could lead into a Bible study or direct your discussion.

1. My greatest fear is....
2. My greatest hope is....
3. The worst thing a person could ever do is....
4. I always get mad when....
5. I always laugh when....
6. I always cry when....
7. If I had a million dollars, I would....
8. I wish my parents would....
9. The President should....
10. My teachers should....
11. Our church should....
12. The happiest day of my life was....
13. The worst day of my life was....
14. The thing I wish I could change....
15. The hardest thing for me to do is....

Wednesday Witness Wear

The youth ministers in one community all encouraged their youth to wear Christian T-shirts to school every Wednesday. This way, kids found out that there were other Christians at their school besides just the ones from their own church.

Yearbook Pages

Buy advertising space in the high school yearbooks in your community. What better way to reach your target audience? You can also advertise in school papers, on band calendars, or on sports bags that the teams sell as fund-raisers.

Youth Group Reunion

Invite past members of the youth group to a reunion party. The current members of the youth group can provide the refreshments and decorations. During the time together, encourage former members of the youth group to share meaningful experiences of their time in the group. Ask them to share the things they remember most about being involved in a youth group. Ask them to give their best advice to members of the current youth group.

Youth Minister Swap

Trade places with another youth minister in your area for a Bible study session. Youth (and youth ministers!) enjoy a new face every once in a while. As long as you are not worried that your group will like the new face better, you are in good shape!

Add Your Own Ideas Here:

_____

_____

_____

_____

_____

_____

_____

_____

Mission and Service Projects

Do you remember learning about astronomy in your eighth grade science class? As long as a star continues to expand its energy outward, it is a healthy star, giving light and heat to the planets orbiting it. But eventually, a star's energy begins to turn inward. When that happens, the star starts to collapse in on itself. Its light grows dimmer, its heat less intense, until it winds up as a black hole. And black holes suck every bit of energy around them into themselves, while giving off none of their own.

This seems to be a pretty good analogy for youth groups that never reach outward to serve anyone else. As long as youth are regularly involved in mission to others, they remain healthy, giving Christ's light and warmth to everyone around them. However, without opportunities for service, youth groups can turn in on themselves, sucking up every resource and draining all your energy.

In this section, you will find lots of good ideas to turn the focus outward in your youth ministries.

Adopt-a-Mile
You have all seen the signs along highways and roads in your area. Some group adopts a stretch of the road and cleans up trash along that mile once a month. But for some reason, you don't often see church names on them. You can change that in your area. Contact the Chamber of Commerce or the highway department to find out more about participating in the program. Youth have an ongoing interest in the environment, so this project would appeal to

them. As a bonus, you get a big green sign with your church youth group's name on it, right next to the road where everyone can see it!

Alternative Home
Provide a place for unwed mothers to go as an abortion alternative, or volunteer time at an existing facility in your area.

Bible Drive
Announce to your congregation that youth will be collecting used Bibles and other Christian literature. Explain that the Bibles and materials will be sent to people who have none. In advance, find out the names of Christian organizations or missionaries needing these materials. After youth have collected the Bibles and literature for several months, take them or send them to the appropriate place.

Camp Agape
First Baptist Church of Cornelia, Georgia, offers this camp for socially challenged children. They rent a nearby retreat center for one week during the summer and involve the entire church in planning, administering, and conducting the camp. Names of children were provided by the Department of Family and Children's Services.

Christmas Child Care
The church provided free child care to the community on the first Saturday in December and the second Friday and Saturday. Youth kept children from 9 a.m.until 5 p.m. while the parents went shopping. They played games, had crafts, and watched movies, but they also worked on a Christmas musical together. The second Sunday night in December, they presented the musical in the evening worship service, and invited all parents. It turned out to be an incredi-

ble outreach event for the community, with several families joining the church because of it.

Christmas in August

A youth ministry had a great time buying new toys and games for a low-income day care center in the middle of the summer. They went to the center, sang Christmas songs with the kids, played games, and had a great time.

Christmas Store at a Nursing Home

Those confined to a nursing facility need to feel that they can still go about some normal routines in society. Get donated items from people in the church and from local businesses. It can be gifts, such as potholders or picture frames, or food, such as fruit baskets or chocolates. Decide on a price for each item. Then distribute play money to the residents. Set up a "store" in one of the halls of the nursing home, and let residents go from table to table, "buying" gifts, either for themselves or for someone else. One table can be a wrapping table where residents can pay a play "dollar" to have their gifts wrapped.

Christmas with a Family

One church sponsored a mission, and the Middle School and High School Departments each adopted a low-income family that attended the mission. They filled the family's wish lists, brought them dinner and a tree, and spent a part of Christmas Day with the family.

Clothing Hunt

This project is like a scavenger hunt and can be done with individuals or in small groups. Give the youth a list of clothing needs furnished by a specific ministry or organization. Contact this group in advance to request this list. Find out which items are needed most by the organization and assign points accordingly. Youth are given the list with point assignments; then they have a designated time period (one or two hours) to go collect the items and accumulate points. They can go to their own homes or door to door in a neighborhood. A typical list might include: jeans, 100,000 points; coats, 500,000 points, shoes, 75,000 points, shirts, 25,000 points, and so forth. Clothing may be used, but items should be clean and in good repair.

Divorce Panel

With the increase of divorce in our society, here is a program that can help your church and community. Ask several youth and adults to serve on your panel. They all need to be in or to have been in a family where a divorce has already taken place. The adults may be divorced or from a family where their parents divorced. One adult moderates the panel and the discussion time. Make sure this person is very sensitive to the members on the panel. Potential discussion questions might include:

1. What were your feelings as you went through the divorce in your family? How have your feelings changed?
2. How has your role in the family changed as a result of the divorce?
3. What kinds of things did friends say or do as a result of the divorce? What do you wish people had said or done?
4. What is the best advice you can give a youth whose parents are going through a divorce?

You can take questions from the audience; the best way is to have the audience write down their questions. The moderator then reads the questions and can screen

out any inappropriate ones. You may choose to include a family counselor on your panel who can address emotional issues and explain the impact divorce has on individuals in a family. Be sure to advertise the divorce panel discussion in your church and community. Many people will want to take advantage of this opportunity. Invite those people in the process of a divorce and those who may be interested in helping friends or extended family members going through a divorce.

Extra Help Saturday

Distribute flyers around specific neighborhoods announcing that a certain Saturday will be "extra help" day for your youth group. Explain in the flyer that on that day the church bus will be driving through the neighborhood and that youth will be ready to give extra help where needed. Any home needing extra help on a project should tie a bandanna onto the doorknob of the front door. Explain that the work is a service project of your youth group and all the work is free. Many people will take advantage of the extra help.

Gleaning

Based on the Biblical principle of the poor collecting the windfall after a harvest, the youth of one church went to an apple orchard and collected fallen apples to give to the hungry. It was an extremely effective part of a hunger awareness retreat.

Homeless Shelter

One church bought several mattresses and on certain nights during the winter months opens the church as a homeless shelter. When you consider how often your church building is vacant throughout the week, many opportunities for ministry arise, especially if your church has a gym and locker rooms. Youth can get involved by preparing meals, collecting blankets from

church members, and leading devotionals on site.

Hot Meals to ICU Waiting Rooms

A sensitive ministry to families of patients in the intensive care unit of the local hospital. The youth brought hot meals directly to the waiting room. Be sure to check with the hospital administration for any restrictions.

In-town Mission Trip

Arrange with five different mission agencies in your area to work a full day at each for one week during the summer. Meet for breakfast and Bible study in the morning before you go to the mission sites. At night, come together for a worship service, with lots of time for testimonies. A variation on this idea: split your group into five mission teams, and let each team go to one of the sites each day. That way the group is able to experience lots of different opportunities.

Do your best to structure this event the same way you would a mission trip out of town. Youth would not leave early to go to soccer practice if you were five hundred miles away, so do not let them do it during this week.

Manna Project

You can contact the Foreign Mission Board to coordinate this project. The youth group is linked to a list of specific needs for a particular missionary. At different times throughout the year, they work on getting those needs met. Since most church youth groups will not go overseas for mission trips, this gives youth a sense of ownership to foreign missions because they have a name to pray for.

Meals on Wheels

One youth group volunteered for a community service project to bring food to shut-ins.

Migrant Workers

Some churches in farming communities have special ministries for seasonal migrant workers. One church began a day care center for the children of migrant workers.

Mini-Camp

A church youth group was so excited when they got back from their *Centrifuge* youth camp, they did a day camp for the children at their church a few weeks later. They played the same games with them, had a similar worship service (where the youth preached and led music). They even made T-shirts for the camp.

This idea could also be adapted to a community service camp format, with teenagers performing various community services upon their return.

Missionary Dinner

Instruct the youth group to select some missionaries who are home for furlough and some who are abroad. Ask youth to plan in advance to cook and serve dinner for those who are on furlough. Youth are to decorate and provide some form of entertainment for the missionaries and try to serve dishes native to the country where the missionaries serve.

For the missionaries who are abroad, youth can send dinner-in-a-box. Youth will collect food items (nonperishables) which can be sent in one box to the missionaries. If possible get a list of items the missionaries like but

cannot get overseas. This project can be done any time of the year. Make sure youth enclose notes of encouragement or a video message from the group.

Nursing Home Beauty Shop

A service project the Acteens really got into. This particular church had a member who was a beautician, who volunteered her time at the nursing home. The Acteens went along, prepping the residents for beauty treatments and spending time with them.

Nursing Home VBS

Many nursing home residents have some of the same developmental needs as children. Vacation Bible School, complete with crafts, Bible stories, songs, and refreshments, can be a wonderful ministry to them.

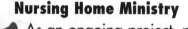

Nursing Home Ministry

As an ongoing project, provide activities for a local nursing home each month. At Christmas, bring Christmas baskets, at Halloween bring Halloween goodies (make sure you check with the dietitian at the home for appropriate candy). A great ministry is to adopt a nursing home resident. Pair up adults with youth, and have youth commit to praying for their residents, writing to them, exchanging photos, and so forth.

Santa's Helpers

During the month of December enlist youth to be "on call" as Santa's Helpers. Youth make themselves available to help families in the church or the community with a variety of activities. Possible Santa's Helpers projects might include: baby-sitting while parents Christmas shop, helping a family decorate their yard or home with lights, helping to bake cookies or bread to be given as gifts, providing a gift wrapping service (families bring their own paper and supplies, youth do the wrapping), or any other related request. The idea is for youth to give their time and talents to other members or the church or community. This activity should not cost the youth or their parents anything financially. This works great if students are out of school for the holidays a week or more before Christmas when families are caught in the Christmas rush to get many things done.

Seniors on Saturdays (SOS)
Senior adults in the church are asked to contact the youth ministry about needs around their houses that youth can fill on Saturday. This has served as a really effective inter-generational relationship builder.

Smoke Alarms
Begin by deciding whether the smoke detectors will be purchased or donated. The local fire marshal's office usually has connections to suppliers who will donate smoke detectors. Usually the group who does the installing just needs to turn in a list of names of where the detectors have been placed. Prepare a list of names or neighborhoods where the smoke detectors may be needed. Ask youth to either call these individuals or go door-to-door to find out who needs the smoke alarms. Arrange a time when a few members of the group would be welcome in the home to install the detector. Explain that the smoke detectors and installation are free, compliments of your church or group.

On the weekends daylight saving begins or ends, everyone is encouraged to check and change the batteries in their smoke detectors. Senior adults may have difficulty climbing up to do this. The youth can call the church's seniors who live in their own homes and ask if they might like to have a youth take care of this. Most adults will supply the batteries, but the youth should have some with them, too.

Teacher Appreciation Banquet

Each youth adopted a teacher at their high school and personally invited him or her to a banquet held at the church. The banquet was simply to say "thanks" for the work the teachers did. It was not overtly evangelistic, but it was designed to show that teachers can, and should, expect something different from their Christian students. This idea would also work for a Police Officer Appreciation Banquet. One youth group raised enough money to purchase a new bulletproof vest for the police department which they presented at the banquet. Both these events went a long way in improving relationships between the church and community.

Trailblazers

One night a week, or one day a week during the summer, do work with inner-city children using a Vacation Bible School format.

Trip Packets

This is a great way to minister to weary travelers stopping through your area. Plan to spend a summer day at a local rest stop or pic-nic area. Ahead of time put together trip packets to give out to travelers. Items in the trip packet might include maps, brochures of local attractions, puzzles, games, Christian music cassette, gum or snacks. These items can be placed inside a paper bag. As travelers arrive at the rest stop, invite children to play organized games led by youth. Offer to clean windshields or help with possible minor car repairs. The idea is for youth to make themselves available to the visitors. Youth can have tracts available or Bibles to share the gospel with the travelers. Use your imagination, and there is no telling what might happen. However, do make sure to ask for permission to provide these services at the rest stop.

Widow/Widower Dinner

The youth group plans, prepares and serves a dinner for the widows and widowers at your church or in the community. After the meal youth provide entertainment—story telling, group singing, games, old movies, and so forth. The youth who are not leading the entertainment can begin to clean up. However, they need to make sure no one feels rushed to leave the event. This can be great fun, and everyone makes new friends.

Windshield Washing

For this project youth will need window cleaner, paper towels, or squeegees. Find a large parking lot filled with cars, like a mall. The youth move up and down the rows of cars cleaning the dirty windshields. Youth then leave a small note with a verse of Scripture or a word of encouragement hoping the driver attends the church of his or her choice next week. Remind youth that this project is done for free; no donations accepted if the owners walk up to their cars at the time the windshields are being cleaned.

Work Day at a Baptist Camp

In the spring, one youth group did major preseason work on the state Baptist camp. They cut grass, repainted, cleaned buildings, washed windows, and so on. Their major project was building a new children's playground

for the camp.

Youth Christmas Party

Charge $3 for youth to come, but that money goes to meet a need in the commu-nity. The group decides in advance where they want the money to go, and at the end of the party they deliver it as a group.

Add Your Own Ideas Here:

_____

_____

_____

_____

_____

_____

_____

_____

_____

_____

_____

_____

_____

_____

_____

_____

_____

_____

_____

_____

_____

_____

_____

_____

Contributors

Jan Adams	Kathy and Dennis Campbell
Anita Agee	Greg Carder
Gary Alley	Ricky Caulder
Dan Anderson	Julie Chapman
David Atkins	Cindy Chappelear
Sue Balderson	John Chipps
Steve Barcik	Bill Coleman
Jim Barnard	Jennifer Combs
Darrin Barth	Sean Conner
Curt Becker	Brady Cooper
Ellis Beddingfield	Patsy Cooper
Jeanie and Jerry Biggs	Pat and Billy Cox
Patti Birchett	Anna Crawford
Russell Black	Joanie and Ed Crawley
Bradley Blackwell	Tim Crawley
Ken Blakney	J. Culver
Herman Bowers	Jim Daniels
Joan Brewster	John Davis
Miles Britt	Sandy Davis
Melissa and Rob Britton	Bill Dennington
Becki Brown	John Dickinson
Pat Brown	Gary Dillard
Jack Bruce	Gary Dover
Andy Buchanan	Laura Drown
Fred Bullock	Roy Dobbss
John Burke	Wanda Ellis
Jeff Buscher	Linda Emmons
Gayle Butler	Billy Ray Ervin
Patricia Butler	Brenda Eubanks

Debbie Fanter
Jennifer Fields
Randy Fields
Blake Foster
Wendell Frazier
Ryan Fuller
Billy Garrett
Glenn Gay
Shelly Gazaway
Kim and Darren George
Tracey Goen
Cathy Gonzalez
Debbie Goodin
Jeffrey Goodreau
JoEllen and Chip Gordon
Remo Gori
Linda Gossett
Pam Gregory
Connie Hale
Daryl Hall
Sharon and Hal Haller
Kathy Haskell
Mary Anne Hayes
Terry Hearen
Amy Hendrix
Gela Hendrix
Mildred Herdejurgen
Paul R. Hickman, Jr.
Sherry Hildebrandt
Terry Hinds
Kathy Hodges
Ken Holcombe
John Hucks
Kathy Hutcherson
Jo Ingram
Virginia Jenkins
Jan Johnson
Neil Johnson
Betty Kay Jordan
Jeff Keas

William Kilgore
Ruth Nell Kinnison
Randy Kirby
Lisa Knight
Joey Lewis
Winnie Little
Gayle Lofton
JoAnne and Keith Longo
Melanie Lowery
Dwayne Lyles
Don Macon
Virginia Martin
Conway Massey
Jeff Maxey
Scott Maze
John McCallister
Annette and Don McClary
Jere McClendon
Ed McGee
Tim McKinley
Melissa McKormick
Sherry McMahane
Mike Medling
Joy Mills
Steve Mills
Ron Mize
David Mobley
Alan Moore
Robby Myrick
Rhea Nethery
Charles Nikolic
Billy Nolen
Jackie Ogles
Gail and Scott Otto
Kathy Owens
Dawn Palmer
Ivan Parke
Don Parker
Denise and Terry Parks
Ken Patterson

Contributors

McKay Pearce
Kirk Pearson
Paula Peek
Connie and Dwight Perry
Michael Perry
Pruette Plemens
Drew Porterfield
Carol and Mike Puckett
Renee Puckett
Sha Purvis
Jeff Randolph
Ted Ray
Julie and Jim Reed
Susan Reed
Angie Reeves
Donnis and Lowell Reichardt
Ted Richards
Vincent Riobo
Elaine Rizor
Cathy Rogers
Pam and Scott Rowlett
Steve Russell
Jimmy Sadler
Ann Sanders
Rhonda Sands
Rick Sellers
Bob Sessoms
Larry Simpson
Allen Sims
Tim Skinner
Acker Smith
Angela Smith
Gregory Spear
Brian Spears
Steve Staneart
Ginny Stewart
Kathy Stratman
Rob Sutton
Jill Swann
Bill Taylor

Jenny Templeton
Sheila Thacker
Campbell Thames
Sherry Thompson
Julie Tilman
Debbie Trapp
Bill Treadway
Dave True
Ray Tucker
Jimmy Veazey
Brad Vose
Randy Wager
Peggy Walker
Virginia Ward
Ann Marie Wells
Angie and Blake Westbrook
Scott Williams
Susan Williams
Ernie Willis
Cheryl Wooten
Mike Young